Heroes Behind the Mask

Ramsha Essa & Mirza Baig

Heroes Behind the Mask

References to studies and other third-party works are cited within this publication. All referenced works are credited to their respective authors.

For permission requests, write to the publisher at the address below:
KDP (Kindle Direct Publishing)
202 Westlake Ave N Ste 2, Seattle, WA 98109-5264.

Visit our website: **www.prehealthshadowing.com**

ISBNs
Ebook: 979-8-9889041-2-0
Paperback: 979-8-9889041-1-3
Hardcover: 979-8-9889041-0-6
Pre-Health Shadowing, Inc.

Cover design: Kai Miller

First Edition: April 2025
Printed in the United States of America

Dedication

To my parents, thank you for always being there and supporting me in everything I do. I'm so grateful for your love and guidance. To all the healthcare professionals who worked tirelessly during the pandemic, you are true heroes. Your dedication and care have made a lasting impact, and this is for you.

—Ramsha Essa

To my wonderful family, thank you for always loving and supporting me. May God bless you.

—Mirza Mustafa Baig

For all who believed in me, taught me something new, or simply stood by my side. Your impact will always be a part of my story.

—Nina Bouzamondo-Bernstein

Table of Contents

Notes from the Authors

This book started with the simple idea of honoring the healthcare professionals who sacrificed to care for their patients. What began as a few pages of words has grown into a book I'm incredibly proud of and excited to share with many.

I thank my co-author and Pre-Health Shadowing (PHS) for their amazing support and guidance in shaping this idea. I also say a heartfelt thank you to all the healthcare professionals who shared their stories and allowed me to be their voice.

—Ramsha Essa

I am grateful you've chosen to read this book. Within these pages, I hope you find wisdom and insights that resonate with you. This book shares untold stories from the pandemic and offers a gentle reminder to pause and reflect on how you spend this precious gift of life. Let it be a soft nudge—a wake-up call—to pursue what truly matters with the time you have left. Be kind, be fair, beware of harshness, and live with integrity. I hope these narratives reinvigorate you to chase what is important and leave what is not.

—Mirza Mustafa Baig

A Note From the CEO of Pre-Health Shadowing

When I founded Pre-Health Shadowing in September 2020, it was a response to a challenge I and many others faced during an incredibly difficult time. As a full-time student working toward a healthcare career, I was ready to gain real-world experience through clinical shadowing. But with the onset of COVID-19, in-person shadowing opportunities vanished almost overnight. The absence of those hands-on experiences felt like a huge setback—not just for me but for thousands of aspiring healthcare professionals around the world. In a health crisis where millions need care, we must uplift the next generation of providers, learn from today's professionals and policies, and listen closely to the pain points to shape what comes next.

That's exactly what led to the creation of Pre-Health Shadowing in September 2020. As a full-time student preparing for a career in healthcare, I, like so many others, faced a sudden loss of access to clinical experiences when the pandemic began. In-person shadowing opportunities disappeared overnight, and what once felt like a clear path forward suddenly became uncertain.

Pre-Health Shadowing was created as a response to that gap, but it has grown into something much more. It's become a platform focused on long-term impact—connecting students to real healthcare professionals, breaking down barriers, and creating space for career exploration and learning that's accessible to all.

Since launching, we've welcomed over 70,000 students from around the world into our community. Our live, interactive sessions with professionals across disciplines don't just help students meet a moment—they help build the foundation for what's next. Through this work, we're contributing to a stronger, more prepared, and more equitable healthcare future—one that's thoughtful, informed, and built to last.

What I'm most proud of is how we've been able to open doors for students who might not have had access to these kinds of opportunities before. Even though life is returning to normal in many ways, and in-person shadowing is resuming for some, Pre-Health Shadowing is still crucial. There are students who, for various reasons, don't have easy access to healthcare environments. Whether it's because of where they live, their financial situation, or a lack of connections in the healthcare field, the barriers to shadowing can be overwhelming. Our platform provides a way to overcome these challenges.

Access to education shouldn't be determined by where you live or who you know. Many students live in rural areas with few healthcare facilities nearby. Others can't afford to take unpaid shadowing opportunities or travel to larger cities where these experiences are more available. Family connections and mentorship can also play a big role in who gets access to healthcare careers. Not everyone has these advantages, and that's why I believe so strongly in what we're doing at PHS.

We're creating a space where every student can explore their interests in healthcare without being held back by factors outside their control. I'm incredibly passionate about making sure that no matter where you come from, you have the opportunity to discover whether healthcare is the right path for you. And more than that, we're helping students gain the knowledge and confidence they need to pursue their dreams, even if they can't do it in the traditional way.

The impact we've made so far is tangible. I've heard countless stories from students who've used our platform to decide on their future careers, find mentors, or gain the experience they needed to apply to healthcare programs. It's these stories that remind me why we do this work. And it's why we're committed to continuing this mission, even as the world shifts back to in-person activities.

Healthcare needs bright, passionate people from all walks of life, and I truly believe Pre-Health Shadowing is helping to build the next generation of healthcare professionals. We're not just filling a gap created by the pandemic; we're laying the foundation for something that will have a long-lasting impact.

As we continue to grow, my vision for PHS is to expand our reach, connect with even more professionals, and ensure that no student is left out of the healthcare conversation. Whether it's through more shadowing sessions, partnerships, or mentorship programs, we're committed to making sure every student has the opportunity to succeed.

Thank you for being a part of this journey and believing in what we're doing. Together, we're making healthcare education more accessible, equitable, and inclusive.

—Nina Bouzamondo-Bernstein
Founder and CEO, Pre-Health Shadowing

Acknowledgments

We extend our heartfelt gratitude to the incredible volunteers who helped make this project a reality. Your dedication, hard work, and passion have been instrumental throughout this journey.

A special thank you to **Nina Bouzamondo-Bernstein,** the founder and CEO of Pre-Health Shadowing, whose leadership and vision guided this project from the very beginning. Nina spearheaded the collaboration, bringing together professionals, volunteers, and contributors from all over the world. Her unwavering dedication to providing opportunities for pre-health students and her commitment to this project were vital to its success. This book is a testament to her tireless efforts to empower and uplift the next generation of healthcare professionals.

A special thank you to **Alina Azmat**, our book coordinator, who truly wore many hats throughout this project. Alina skillfully communicated with our professionals, authors, and volunteers, ensuring everyone stayed connected and on track. She played an integral role in public relations, marketing, and project management, keeping the project moving forward at every stage. This project would not have been possible without her unwavering dedication, meticulous attention to detail, and outstanding leadership.

We are also incredibly grateful to **May Rajtboriraks** for leading a talented team of volunteers and designing all of the visual content. Her creativity and vision brought this project to life through compelling visuals that capture its essence.

Thank you to the **PHS Leadership Team** for their ongoing support and guidance throughout this process. Special recognition goes to present and past members **Jane Ton**, **Natalie Zimmerman**, and **Jason Braun** for their leadership, commitment, and contributions to the growth and success of this project and Pre-Health Shadowing as a whole.

We also want to thank **Eric Lindberg** and **Jennifer Abayowa**, our editors, for ensuring the content was polished and professional. Your keen eye and thoughtful edits helped shape the final product. **Kai Miller**, our talented cover designer, deserves special recognition for creating a visually stunning cover that perfectly represents the heart of this project.

To our amazing volunteers who contributed their time and skills:

- **Maria Mina** – Assisted with Instagram social media logistics and posting, ensuring the project's online presence was well-coordinated and engaging.
- **Ameera Khan** – Assisted with Instagram social media logistics and posting, including scheduling posts and monitoring the account, amplifying the project outreach efforts.
- **Tatiana Cuebas-Hernandez** – Assisted with TikTok social media logistics and posting, including participating in content creation and overseeing the app, amplifying the project outreach efforts.
- **Hafia Uddin** – Supported various tasks, offering valuable help in different project areas.

- **Ashley Shen** – Provided crucial support throughout the project, helping to ensure smooth progress in multiple aspects.
- **Emma McGahan** – Helped manage social media content, amplifying the project's outreach and engagement.
- **Charlie Sconiers** – Dedicated time to internal communication and logistics, ensuring clear and effective coordination across the team.
- **Ayem Mokhtabad** – Played a key role in community outreach and public relations, helping to spread the word about the project.
- **Muntaha Islam** – Supported internal communication and public relations, enhancing the team's workflow and external presence.
- **Divyaprasanna Udumula** – Contributed to internal communication and logistics, assisting with behind-the-scenes coordination.
- **Isra Ahmed** – Worked on content creation, including images and blog article writing, enhancing the project's visibility through written and visual content.
- **Eva Lo** – Assisted with blog article writing, contributing thoughtful and engaging content to the project's narrative.
- **Arya Panda** – Focused on content creation, particularly images, helping to represent the project visually.
- **Hans Loja** – Played an essential role in community outreach, expanding the project's reach within various networks.

- **Verisha Bhatti** – Provided valuable support in various tasks, contributing to the project's overall success.
- **Ziwen Qian** – Played a key role in social media content creation alongside outreach-related tasks, contributing greatly to our marketing team and its success.
- **Aabha Vadapalli** – Contributed to various sub-departments within this project, including marketing and public relations.
- **Fatima Lookmanji-Khan** – Dedicated several hours to article creation for the Pre-Health Shadowing blog page concerning the project and its connection to bigger health topics.
- **Abinaya Sridharan** – Dedicated various hours to marketing and public relations, gathering several contacts for our team to grow and publicize this project.
- **Adriana Camila Crespo** – A member of our research team, gathering sources for our co-authors to elevate the stories within each chapter.
- **Armaanjit Singh** – A member of our research team, gathering statistical sources to elevate specific chapters and their connections to real-world situations.
- **Kevin Brian** – A member of the research team, efficiently and promptly locating research papers to elevate the book's content.
- **Melody Lemus** – A member of the research team, dedicated to finding credible sources to elevate the book's themes.

- **Gehna Srivastava** – Dedicated several hours to marketing, including assistance with social media, outreach, and research.
- **Fatima Atieh** – Played an essential role in the research team, finding research about the book's themes to elevate the written content.
- **Yulia Dubrovensky** – A member of our content creator team who effectively contributed to developing social media content for the greater community.
- **Sidona Berhe** – A dedicated member of our content creator team who worked diligently in a fast-paced environment to develop reels for our social media pages.
- **Ayesha Haider** – A team member of our content creator team, ready to take on multiple tasks to support this project, including to develop multiple reels for social media.
- **Enoch Gurah Ansoh** – A valuable member of our content creator team who rapidly and accurately developed several reels within a short timeframe.

We would also like to recognize our wonderful beta readers: **Dr. Gbemisola Daniyan**, **Dr. Jane Parker**, **Jerry Elprin**, and **Dylan Greany**. Your thoughtful feedback, attention to detail, and support have been crucial in refining the final version of this work. We are deeply grateful for your insights and contributions.

A sincere thanks to **Dr. Sunshine (Sunny) Nakae**, a valued Pre-Health Shadowing Advisory Board member. Your unwavering support and belief in this project have been a source of inspiration, and your guidance has been instrumental in shaping its success.

To all who have contributed in big and small ways, thank you for your commitment to this project. We are truly grateful to have worked alongside such a dedicated and passionate team.

Introduction

This book is a tribute to the millions of friends we lost due to the 2019 Coronavirus disease pandemic (COVID-19), including our frontline workers who put themselves in danger daily, their families, and all those who persevered through the pandemic.

It aims to provide a general understanding of COVID-19, which affected every inch of the globe, and highlights the pandemic's impact on our courageous frontline heroes. It will share stories of medical providers, such as physicians, physician assistants (PAs), nurses, emergency medical technicians (EMTs), certified nursing assistants (CNAs), nurse practitioners (NPs), health technicians, and various valued healthcare workers, to help us learn about their experiences and express our gratitude for their efforts and sacrifices. We begin with a brief overview of Coronaviruses.

Coronaviruses are a family of viruses, named by their appearance and known to affect the respiratory tracts of humans and animals, causing symptoms similar to the flu and common cold.[1] The older coronaviruses, identified in the 1900s, caused a milder respiratory infection, while viruses in the 2000s caused a more severe infection. As decades passed, they infected new hosts and acquired new modifications known as mutations. With each mutation, they grew and changed into a new virus, finding ways to become

[1] National Institute of Allergy and Infectious Diseases. Coronaviruses [Internet]. 2024 July 31. Available from: https://www.niaid.nih.gov/diseases-conditions/coronaviruses

increasingly pathogenic or capable of causing disease.[2] While mutating, they jumped into new hosts, other animals, and then humans, and presented in more severe outbreaks worldwide, like the infamous coronavirus disease 2019, abbreviated as COVID-19. The coronavirus responsible for the COVID-19 pandemic is the severe acute respiratory syndrome coronavirus-2, abbreviated as SARS-CoV-2.

SARS-CoV-2 is not the only coronavirus that has prompted a concerning outbreak. The severe acute respiratory syndrome coronavirus-1 (SARS-CoV-1) outbreak of 2002 and the Middle East respiratory syndrome coronavirus (MERS-CoV) outbreak of 2012 were also responsible for causing widespread panic. SARS-CoV-1 emerged in China and was discovered after a case of atypical illness was reported in the Guangdong province in southern China.[3] A relative of this virus, MERS-CoV, emerged in the Middle East and caused another outbreak.[4]

We extracted the information above from credible sources. To write the following chapters, we interviewed medical professionals and collected their narratives. Using digital media, we documented their accounts, stories, and experiences. As we conducted interviews, we were moved by the many stories that went unheard, those depicting loss,

---

[2] Kahn JS, McIntosh K. History and Recent Advances in Coronavirus Discovery. Pediatric Infectious Disease Journal. 2005 Nov;24(11):S223–7.

[3] Cherry JD, Krogstad P. SARS: the first pandemic of the 21st century. Pediatr Res. 2004 Jul;56(1):1–5.

[4] Al-Osail AM, Al-Wazzah MJ. The history and epidemiology of Middle East respiratory syndrome corona virus. Multidiscip Respir Med. 2017;12:20.

triumph, and hope, and we are excited to share them with you. We hope that as you read this book, you gain a greater appreciation for our frontline workers and a deeper understanding of the catastrophic nature of the COVID-19 pandemic.

Part 1: The Frontline Experience

Sacrifices, Triumphs, and Systemic Failures

Introduction

In the early days of the pandemic, many of us felt like we were trapped in a dystopian narrative—one where each day oscillated between hope and uncertainty, as if we stood on the edge of an ending we couldn't yet see. The world of healthcare, in particular, transformed overnight. Hospitals became battlegrounds, clinics turned into makeshift command centers, and telemedicine emerged as an unlikely hero. This introduction sets the stage for an exploration of those turbulent times, weaving together personal stories, system-wide challenges, and the groundbreaking research that helped redefine our approach to care.

When the virus first spread, the fear was palpable. The Centers for Disease Control and Prevention (CDC) reported a significant increase in telehealth usage during the early stages of the COVID-19 pandemic. Specifically, there was a 154% increase in telehealth visits during the last week of March 2020 compared to the same period in 2019.[5] Virtual consultations soared as patients sought safe alternatives to in-person visits, a move that not only redefined convenience but also highlighted deep-seated inequalities in access to healthcare. The rapid adoption of telemedicine, supported by data from studies published by the National Institutes of Health (NIH), suggested that even brief interactions—a mere two to three minutes—could effectively address low-acuity

[5] Centers for Disease Control and Prevention. This Week in MMWR – October 30, 2020. MMWR Morb Mortal Wkly Rep. 2020 Oct 30;69(43):1403–4.

complaints, freeing up precious time and resources for those in critical need.[6]

Yet behind these promising numbers lay deeper, more complex realities. Healthcare professionals in both rural and urban communities faced unprecedented emotional and logistical challenges. They struggled to balance the demands of their daily roles with severe staff shortages, heightened stress, and the constant threat of exposure. These pressures exposed the vulnerabilities of a healthcare system stretched to its limits, highlighting broader systemic issues that affected providers worldwide.

This narrative is more than a discussion of statistics or technological shifts—it's an exploration of the lived experiences within healthcare during a crisis. From the brief moments of relief and camaraderie within vaccine clinics to the quiet solidarity during morning briefings, healthcare teams navigated intense circumstances marked by difficult decisions and profound responsibility. In critical care environments, the urgency and gravity of these choices emphasized the deeply human aspect of caregiving—showcasing the courage, resilience, and dedication required from those tasked with caring for others amid uncertainty and risk.

The Washington Post and The New York Times also highlighted the ethical and practical dilemmas faced by healthcare providers during the pandemic—dilemmas that forced providers to balance the hope of technological

[6] Smith AC, Thomas E, Snoswell CL, Haydon H, Mehrotra A, Clemensen J, Caffery LJ. Telehealth for global emergencies: Implications for coronavirus disease 2019 (COVID-19). J Telemed Telecare. 2020 May;26(5):309–13.

innovation with the limitations of a system that was not fully prepared for such an onslaught. For emergency room residents and seasoned physicians alike, the tension between the expectation to save everyone and the harsh reality of limited resources became an everyday battle. The emotional toll was profound, with many healthcare workers recounting how long shifts and the constant fear of exposure led to burnout, anxiety, and, in some cases, irreversible changes in their outlook on patient care.

Across the chapters of this book, we journey through varied landscapes of the pandemic: from the early days of telemedicine and makeshift vaccine clinics to the critical care scenarios where every moment was a race against time, from the raw, unfiltered experiences of emergency room residents to the reflective narratives of anesthesiologists who witnessed both the fragility and resilience of the human body. Each chapter is a window into a world where personal courage met systemic challenges, where every story was a blend of heartbreak and hope.

Research from the NIH reinforces the significance of these experiences. Studies have shown that the mental health impact on healthcare workers was not merely anecdotal; there was a measurable increase in anxiety, depression, and insomnia—conditions exacerbated by the physical barriers imposed by personal protective equipment (PPE) and the relentless pace of clinical work.[7] The CDC, too, has pointed to the need for systemic changes in how we approach public health crises, advocating for stronger support systems that

[7] Biber J, Ranes B, Lawrence S, Malpani V, Trinh TT, Cyders A, English S, Staub CL, McCausland KL, Kosinski M, Baranwal N, Berg D, Pop R. Mental health impact on healthcare workers due to the COVID-19 pandemic: a U.S. cross-sectional survey study. J Patient Rep Outcomes. 2022 Jun 13;6:63.

could prevent the kind of burnout witnessed in countless hospitals across the country

In the following chapters, we will delve into specific experiences—from the poignant story of a physician juggling the demands of an overburdened practice, to the heart-wrenching dilemmas faced in critical care, to the raw realities of life in an overwhelmed emergency room, and finally, to the nuanced reflections of an anesthesiologist on the frontlines of surgical care. Each narrative is a reflection of a broader societal crisis and a celebration of the resilience that emerged amidst unprecedented challenges.

This introduction, much like the first steps into a new chapter of life, invites you to pause and reflect on the complex interplay of fear, hope, and innovation that defined the early days of the pandemic. It is an invitation to understand that, even in our darkest moments, there lies the potential for great change—a change driven by empathy, collaboration, and the pursuit of better care. As you read on, remember that the challenges described here are not isolated incidents but rather threads woven into the fabric of a healthcare system in transition, a system that continues to learn and evolve in the face of new threats.

The first section is structured to reflect the evolving challenges and responses throughout the pandemic, following the experiences of healthcare providers as they navigated a crisis. It begins with the initial wave of uncertainty, capturing the fear, confusion, and rapid changes that swept through hospitals and clinics. From there, it shifts to the height of the pandemic, where the emotional and ethical weight on frontline workers intensified—ICUs overflowed, burnout spread, and tensions between patients and providers escalated. Finally, the focus turns to adaptation and resilience, exploring how healthcare professionals adjusted to new realities through innovations like telemedicine and reimagined approaches to patient care. While each chapter presents a unique perspective, together they offer a powerful, multifaceted look at how medicine was reshaped in a time of crisis.

By exploring these intertwined narratives and supporting research, we aim to present not just a chronicle of events, but a deeper understanding of how these moments reshaped our collective approach to healthcare. This is a story of crisis and renewal—a narrative that highlights the importance of resilience, innovation, and above all, the human connection in times of unparalleled uncertainty.

We Were Crying and Laughing, and It Felt Like the Beginning of the End

I used to say when I read the last book in the Harry Potter series, I had to turn to the end of the book and find out if Harry Potter lived—and I kept saying I wished I could turn to the end of the pandemic and find out if I am going to live because it felt like a very serious and scary threat.

Despite being in the middle of the pandemic, Dr. Katherine Atkinson, a family medicine physician, still ran her successful family practice in Northampton, MA. Like so many physicians across the country, she was struggling to keep pace with the sweeping changes in healthcare. In larger hospitals, entire wards had shifted to treat COVID-19 cases, and smaller practices like hers were left scrambling for resources—both human and financial. Suddenly, the local family doctor found herself on the front lines of a worldwide crisis, forced to adapt faster than ever before. She found herself stressed juggling her responsibilities. She struggled to balance her duties as a physician and entrepreneur after temporarily losing staff members to periods of self-quarantine.

Dr. Atkinson began to search for new employees to fill positions at her office and meet the growing demands of sick patients. However, she did not receive many applications because people feared contracting the lethal virus. Consequently, her current employees worked more to compensate for the staff shortage. As a result, they felt burnt out, leading some to quit their jobs and leave Dr. Atkinson worried about the future.

Initially, we were all terrified that we were going to catch COVID-19—that we were going to die and people we knew were going to die.

Unfortunately, a lack of primary care physicians in a rural place like Northampton can lead to a significant problem of having underserved populations. This issue can be catastrophic for communities, especially during a pandemic. These were often older adults on limited incomes, families who faced transportation barriers, and individuals struggling with chronic conditions like diabetes or heart disease. Many didn't have easy access to hospitals or specialists, relying on local practices like Dr. Atkinson's for their fundamental medical needs. In a pandemic, this vulnerability became even starker, as even routine checkups and ongoing treatments were suddenly harder to schedule. Additionally, having underserved populations can have dire consequences for future generations within a certain region.

When an underserved population with medical conditions goes without medical intervention for decades, it can affect their children and children's children through stressors, dietary habits, and environmental conditions. This lack of medical intervention can also damage their quality of life, causing a harmful domino effect in the future. And being in a pandemic only exacerbates this problem. Because many family practices around Northampton did not have sufficient staffing to care for locals during the pandemic, any underserved population with unmet medical needs had a greater chance of developing severe progressive conditions and suffering for generations to come.

Dr. Atkinson began to think of a solution to relieve the fears of her employees about contracting the virus from exposed patients. Despite the overwhelming nature of her work, she began to use telehealth visits to minimize the spread of COVID-19, allowing patients a new way to seek health care from home.

Still, many avoided seeking treatment due to additional fees. In certain regions, depending on insurance plans, a co-pay, an out-of-pocket expense for patients to receive health care services, was required to see a doctor. Fortunately, in Massachusetts, co-pays were not applied to telemedicine visits, which opened the doors for a new subset of patients to seek treatment for chronic diseases. Hence, amid an influx of patients and the shortage of staff, while overseeing care for thousands of patients, Dr. Atkinson worried about the viability of her practice. Despite 11 providers, 60 employees, and two offices in a rural area, she feared her practice might shut down. "Patients who met specific, low-risk criteria for one of five different complaints (for example, upper respiratory tract infection, or URI, emergency contraception, conjunctivitis, pharyngitis, and UTIs) had overall low rates of in-office follow-up (about 13.5% of the entire cohort), and less than 1% used emergency services. The e-visits took about two to three minutes of clinician time, suggesting this could be a very cost-effective and efficient intervention for common low-acuity complaints."[8,9]

These studies showed that telemedicine visits for low-risk patients for certain complaints, such as the common cold, the need for emergency contraception, or a urinary tract infection (UTI), required just two to three minutes, saving the need for a more extended visit and commute.

Dr. Atkinson quickly noticed some disadvantages after implementing telemedicine, a digital system that provides medical care from a distance. Unfortunately, there were times when diagnoses were delayed because of telemedicine's restrictive qualities. Once, a patient scheduled a telehealth visit to discuss a growing mass on her neck. During the virtual visit, it looked like a swollen lymph node. When Dr. Atkinson saw the patient in person after a few months, it had grown into a large lump, and she diagnosed it as a tumor. The enlarged tumor was much more challenging to manage and treat than in its earlier stages of development.

It is unsettling to think about the outcomes for patients whose conditions went undiagnosed during the lockdown. They stayed home to protect themselves from a deadly disease, only to be overpowered by another and lose their lives. As strong as we are, it can be excruciatingly painful to endure the loss of a loved one. It can be agonizing to realize that people here yesterday are gone today. These thoughts

---

[8] Shaver J. The State of Telehealth Before and After the COVID-19 Pandemic. Prim Care. 2022 Dec;49(4):517–30.

[9] Bhargava R, Gayre G, Huang J, Sievers E, Reed M. Patient e-Visit Use and Outcomes for Common Symptoms in an Integrated Health Care Delivery System. JAMA Netw Open. 2021 Mar 24;4(3):e212174.

can overwhelm us. They can prevent us from thinking clearly and result in depression and anxiety. They can disrupt our daily productivity and change our routines.

To ease her team's anxieties and stress, Dr. Atkinson started a 15-minute morning huddle with her medical providers at 8 a.m., which was "*the best thing they've ever done.*" Each morning, they took a few moments to chat, show support for one another, and recharge for the new day. People would come to the huddle even on their days off, showing how well Dr. Atkinson organized such an uplifting and encouraging environment. She understood the pandemic's impact on the team and found ways to lighten their mental stress and improve their moods.

Unfortunately, Dr. Atkinson also struggled with her share of mental stress and anxieties during the pandemic, especially when her elderly mother had to isolate herself for a year. Due to her advanced age and weakened immune system, her mother was advised—like many other older people—to remain isolated. Additionally, older adults often have underlying health conditions like heart disease, diabetes, or respiratory issues that can worsen the effects of the virus. Faced with her mother's situation, she couldn't help but think of her older patients who were also isolated at home and battling conditions like cancer and cardiovascular disease. Overwhelmed with these thoughts, Dr. Atkinson realized that they were taking a mental toll on her. She combated this mental stress by action – establishing vaccine clinics in an effort to provide hope for the future.

Every time we conducted vaccine clinics, it boosted the community's morale. For many of these people, it was the first time they'd seen another human in person in a long time. We were crying and laughing, and it felt like it was the beginning of the end. They were the best days of my life—they were so wonderful.

I was desperately in need of hope. In those days, I brought my mother and father-in-law to receive the vaccination, and they were all sobbing. When I gave my mother her first shot, I told her that I would be able to hug her again after six weeks.

The vaccine clinics proved to be a source of hope for people in the community. After living in isolation for so long, they were happy to see others in person and erupted in a sea of emotions. The pandemic had taken a mental toll on them, and those moments marked the beginning of newfound optimism. Several weeks after Dr. Atkinson had administered the vaccine to her mother, she was relieved she could finally hug her again.

Despite the joy of administering vaccines, Dr. Atkinson knew she had a limited time before the vaccine supply ran out, and people might start blaming healthcare workers for the shortage. She described how the governor of Massachusetts distributed vaccines to doctor's offices, which helped prevent the transmission of COVID-19. Unfortunately, Dr. Atkinson didn't have enough vaccines for her patients, so those who still needed them flooded healthcare providers with questions about availability.

Many people were calling the office and begging for vaccines. While everyone was experiencing a pandemic, each person felt like they were the only one who was, so they yelled at my staff. You can only be yelled at so many times before you decide you don't need this anymore.

In response to her community's concerns, Dr. Atkinson tracked down another supply of vaccines and organized a vaccination clinic geared toward children. She and her team had children line up in the parking lot to get their COVID-19 vaccines and laid out balloons and prizes, encouraging families to celebrate the achievement of receiving a vaccine. They turned the clinic into a socially distanced vaccine party to promote the vaccine and educate children on preventing the spread of the virus. Like the previous vaccination clinics, this day brought hope and optimism.

On her journey toward instilling hope, Dr. Atkinson persevered by running her practice during the pandemic despite her overbearing responsibilities to manage her medical center and recruit staff while finding ways to uplift herself and the dispirited community. With the help of her team, she organized events and cheered up disheartened patients while educating them about the virus and vaccine.

As a primary care physician, Dr. Atkinson emphasizes the importance of developing relationships with patients. She has been a thriving force in her community, practicing family medicine, treating conditions in her office, and developing meaningful relationships for over 20 years. She has also adapted to unexpected situations and instilled hope in her patients, friends, and family, persisting through the challenges of the pandemic. Her selfless nature as a healthcare provider shines through her strong support for her patients and their families.

The City That Never Sleeps

We followed the guidelines, and that's all you really can do. We cleaned every single room immediately after each patient interaction. There was no handshaking or contact of any kind. We checked everyone's temperature and tried to limit the spread of the virus. It was about being safe and making patients feel safe. In podiatry, a good number of our patients are elderly, and these people are highly susceptible to contracting COVID-19, so any mistake in following guidelines can lead to a serious issue.

The urban hub of America, filled with the hustle and bustle, heavy foot traffic, complex transportation routes, and people from every corner of the world, is the city that never sleeps—New York City. Unfortunately, when the quarantine struck in March 2020, the hustle and bustle nearly disappeared—foot traffic quieted, medical offices and other businesses shut down, and the city appeared to fall asleep. New York City was beginning to see a structural change. During this crisis, Dr. Mohammad Rimawi, a board-certified podiatrist, like many others found himself seeing patients through telehealth appointments rather than in person.

After adjusting to life in the pandemic and seeing patients online, Dr. Rimawi quickly realized the limitations of not seeing patients in person. In podiatry, much of the diagnostic process relies on hands-on evaluation and real-time observation of the way a person walks or stands—details that can be missed during a virtual visit. Even simple issues like nail thickness, skin temperature, or subtle swelling require physical contact to assess accurately.

Without access to in-office imaging or the ability to directly examine a sore area, Dr. Rimawi often found himself limited in both diagnosis and immediate treatment, which added frustration for him and his patients alike. Along with managing the difficulties of telemedicine, there was an overwhelming concern about the virus spreading among healthcare workers. As vaccines were introduced and the spread of the virus became more under control, there was comfort in knowing that a vaccine was available and that people could now be more immune to the virus. However, the government did not initially mandate all healthcare workers to receive the vaccine, meaning they could easily transmit the virus to another coworker if infected. It wasn't until January 4th, 2022—nearly 22 months after the United States first acknowledged COVID-19 as a national crisis—that the federal government mandated full vaccination for healthcare workers in Medicare- and Medicaid-funded facilities.[10]

In my practice, I had colleagues who did not have issues agreeing to the vaccine and taking precautions. However, I heard some healthcare workers refusing to get the vaccine.

Preventing exposure in the workplace was already tricky, and worrying about unvaccinated staff made it even more difficult. A lack of medical supplies was not helpful, and equipment was scarce and overpriced, but necessary to maintain the safety of staff and potential patients.

[10] Centers for Medicare & Medicaid Services. Biden-Harris Administration Issues Emergency Regulation Requiring COVID-19 Vaccination for Health Care Workers [Internet]. 2021 Nov 4. Available from: https://www.cms.gov/newsroom/press-releases/biden-harris-administration-issues-emergency-regulation-requiring-covid-19-vaccination-health-care

The reasons behind the resistance were complex. Some healthcare providers were uneasy about the vaccine's rapid development and emergency use authorization, feeling that it hadn't been tested as thoroughly as vaccines developed under normal circumstances. Others were more focused on personal health risks, citing worries about side effects and the long-term implications of a new vaccine—even as scientific evidence continued to support its safety. Additionally, there was a subset of people that viewed vaccine mandates as an infringement on personal freedoms, arguing that even in the medical field, individual choice should be respected.

This mix of scientific skepticism, personal fear, and a strong belief in individual autonomy created a challenging environment. The debate over vaccination added another layer of difficulty to an already strained effort to safeguard both healthcare workers and patients during the pandemic. Even as we grappled with internal debates, an external shortage of crucial supplies became evident.

There needed to be more supplies. There were certain times I was paying large amounts for N-95 masks. I once paid $60 for three of them. I was on a community board forum to see who received a shipment of supplies so we could quickly buy supplies from them. I was paying out of my pocket.

This scramble for personal protective equipment (PPE) was a common thread across the nation. In a city as massive as New York, one would expect easy access to supplies—but during the peak of COVID-19, even well-established hospitals struggled to source enough masks, gloves, and gowns. Private practices like Dr. Rimawi's, often operating on slimmer budgets, felt the pinch acutely. Without adequate PPE, the risk of virus transmission soared, creating an impossible choice for physicians: pay exorbitant prices to keep themselves and their patients safe, or close their doors until supplies became available. In a city where healthcare providers serve millions, a single closed practice could have long-reaching consequences for community health.

Unfortunately, here we are years later, looking at old videos of ourselves and seeing how we used to gather without masks, which we find unusual. We have become used to this lifestyle—we take these things for granted.

With these growing challenges, Dr. Rimawi was unsure what the future would hold. Like most others, he assumed the quarantine would last only a few weeks, after which normal life would resume. However, as the weeks turned into months—and eventually years—healthcare providers everywhere faced deeper issues than being released from lockdown. They found themselves needing new skills and training to handle the changing demands of patient care and the long-term effects of COVID-19. Podiatrists like Dr. Rimawi struggled with remote consultations that made hands-on care nearly impossible, while others—such as critical-care-trained anesthesiologists—also faced gaps in knowledge for long-term patient care. An article published by Jarrett et al. (2022) analyzing New York's early pandemic response underscores that many healthcare providers were unable to refine crucial competencies—especially when rapidly redeployed to unfamiliar roles. In particular, staff trained in critical care or anesthesiology faced gaps in caring for long-term, intubated patients, highlighting how reliance on "just-in-time training" fell short during unprecedented surges. These shortfalls in core competencies and technical capacity had a domino effect on patient outcomes and underscored the urgent need for more robust, proactive approaches to workforce education and support.[11]

Not all ambulatory or elective surgery staff had the appropriate skill sets. Even critical care–trained anesthesiologists had knowledge and training gaps in caring for long-term, intubated patients. Although these issues were resolved, they caused a lag in the availability of competent staff and showed that just-in-time training does not always meet urgent staffing needs.

When physicians pivoted to telemedicine during the pandemic, it exposed their constant need for upskilling. Doctors accustomed to in-person patient visits needed to navigate unfamiliar technology platforms. They had to learn to troubleshoot technical issues from scratch while providing empathetic, effective care. They needed to build trust through a screen.

Dr. Rimawi's challenges mirrored what we saw in the study about critical-care-trained anesthesiologists: healthcare providers needed to learn quickly or risk compromising care quality. The learning was complex: conducting virtual assessments, utilizing remote monitoring tools, and navigating digital patient communication. Many

---

[11] Jarrett M, Garrick R, Gaeta A, Lombardi D, Mayo R, McNulty P, et al. Pandemic Preparedness: COVID-19 Lessons Learned in New York's Hospitals. The Joint Commission Journal on Quality and Patient Safety. 2022 Sep;48(9):475–91.

physicians rose to the challenge. Dr. Rimawi's experience showed that ongoing skill development is critical. It also highlighted the need for systemic support to prepare healthcare providers for future crises.

Thrown Into the Fire

As a student, you read twenty different patient studies and come up with the best answers to the case study questions. If your answers are wrong, no worries. You are amending mistakes, which is part of the learning process. No harm done. But the moment you become a resident, everything changes. Suddenly, a single decision can have life-altering consequences for an actual patient, and the stakes feel immeasurably higher. Even though you are still learning, you are expected to make accurate decisions for your patients, usually without time to think it through and use external references. There might not even be enough time to seek an expert's opinion from a senior physician.

Imagine being an emergency room resident, fresh out of medical school and still in the first stages of training, suddenly pushed into patient care during the COVID-19 pandemic. Even though the pandemic has presented unique challenges for everyone, it was quite a nightmarish ride for many residents. The surge of COVID-19 cases forced residents to shift their attention away from a broad range of conditions—like asthma and heart failure, which they were scheduled to study—and instead focus almost exclusively on managing the virus on the front lines. This intense demand on their time left significant gaps in the broader medical training they needed.

How many patients will die from the virus today? Will I be infected next? Despite the hundreds of people I encounter daily, is this protective gear enough to prevent me from catching the virus? Questions like these likely pulsed in residents' minds as they prepared for the day, drove to work, and toiled away. As an emergency room resident, getting sick isn't only a personal setback—it also hurts colleagues. If they became ill, they would be out for 10 to 14 days in the best-case scenario. During that time, their colleagues would likely be overworked, increasing their workload. Feeling burnt out like never before, healthcare workers began to quit for some time to give their minds and bodies a break.

Dr. Adam Goodcoff, Emergency Medicine Resident and CEO of The Med Life and MedFluencers, shed light on many struggles he and his co-workers faced in these unpredictable times.

We saw COVID-19 cases every day in the ICU I worked in. I trusted the protective equipment and colleagues in this case. My colleagues, such as nurses and other physicians, were still standing and performing their duties. I remember going 10–-12 hours on a shift without removing my mask from my face. I had a sore on my nose because one of my masks did not fit my face well. Unfortunately, that was the only mask available, and I had no choice except to wear it.

A few years ago, manufacturers designed masks and gloves for single use. Many physicians would wear a mask to see a patient with a contagious condition and instantly remove it after leaving the room. They would don a new mask if they visited the same patient later. These once-standard practices regarding infectious diseases proved to be luxuries. As COVID-19 cases outpaced expectations, protective gear suddenly became valuable—a means to survive. Many facilities faced a massive shortage of gowns, masks, and other protective items, so they had to preserve their existing equipment and clean used surgical masks as needed. For Dr. Goodcoff, masks were precious in his day-to-day work experience.

When there were supplies, we were allowed to take one mask per day. I would take one mask every day and wear it for the rest of the shift. If I somehow went without seeing a COVID patient for the whole day, I would keep that mask aside because it was considered relatively clean or new. I could use it safely at any other time. I would wear my exposed COVID masks until they were visibly soiled and damaged. Many times, the stripes of the mask would break or wear down, but we were relying 100 % on these masks.

Dr. Goodcoff and many other healthcare workers in his hospital used air-purifying devices or fan systems that created positive pressure around a health provider's head. They serve as a filtration system that cleans all particles in the air and prevents anything from entering the helmet. Although the purifying devices were helpful, they kept healthcare providers from accomplishing a sacred part of their job: engaging with their patients.

Along with the new implementation of air purifying devices, health workers still contracted COVID-19 infection whilst being vaccinated. This caused panic among staff members. Some nurses and physicians in the emergency department lost their lives due to COVID-19, devastating their family and friends.

The way I handled it—I was trying to be in the room as little as possible. It's nice to comfort someone, but at a time early on when we had no vaccine and no understanding of how to treat COVID-19, and people were dying left and right, you had to make certain decisions. Spending an extra 5 or 10 minutes with the patients was not feasible, putting their and our lives at risk. The longer you spend around someone with COVID-19, even with the mask on, the higher your exposure, the more likely you will get COVID-19. One common theme among all physicians was to diagnose patients thoroughly and develop a treatment plan for the patient in as little time as possible.

Even though COVID-19 brought many adversities, it also brought people closer and solidified healthcare workers' reliance on each other. When a nurse or patient care technician became overwhelmed with work and struggled to complete their responsibilities, a physician would support them. Everyone in the community stood by each other in these troubling moments.

We would wipe someone's face shield because they were sweating, help someone replace their mask, quickly switch, and do compressions on a patient because someone's mask strap broke. We were stepping in to fill the void wherever we could. There was a time when a nurse was doing CPR, and her ID bounced on her face shield and around her body. It was swinging. I remember switching out from her to do CPR on the patient because her ID began to pull away from her face shield. It was putting her at a greater risk. People's goggles were falling off, and I was trying to put them back on their faces as they were doing compressions.

Dr. Goodcoff was more than a doctor to his patients—he became a source of unity for his colleagues, stepping up as both a mentor and educator during an unprecedented crisis.

Between hospital shifts, he used his social media platform, The Med Life, to share real-time updates from the front lines, offering practical tips and firsthand glimpses of what it was like to battle COVID-19 each day.

I was very fortunate to grow my audience during this time. I made content surrounding vaccines. There were many anti-vaccine individuals. A lot of people were scared of getting the COVID-19 vaccine. I had a video taken of me when I got the first vaccination. It was a student nurse who gave me that shot. I did not disclose where I got the shot from. I did not talk about anyone in the video. You could only see the side of the student nurse's face, so one could not recognize her from the video. Somebody was watching the video and knew who that student nurse was. He sent the video to her, and she commented, expressing her gratitude for sharing the video. It became clear that I have the reach and my content makes a difference, which motivated me to make more content that can help educate people.

Dr. Adam Goodcoff was just trying to keep his head above water—managing a daily flood of patients in an overwhelmed emergency room, asking himself if he could make it through another shift. However, there was another crisis brewing beyond the hospital walls. People locked at home, glued to their phones, spun in circles by half-truths and confusion about COVID-19. They didn't know where to turn. He saw it plainly: the pandemic wasn't just a battle fought in exam rooms. It was also a scramble for clear, trusted information.

He had only a phone and a social media account to work with, but sometimes that's all it takes. Between shifts—still wearing his scrubs, maybe an aching lower back from hours on his feet—he recorded quick videos in hallways, parking lots, or his cluttered apartment. He walked viewers through masking basics, how vaccines worked, and what the data really meant. With each post, he cut through the fog just a little, meeting people where they lived: on their screens, at home, anxious for answers.

Dr. Goodcoff found himself stepping outside the usual bounds of a resident's life. He wasn't just treating patients or charting vitals; he was also speaking directly to everyone else, turning confusion into something real and understandable. It wasn't glamorous—his phone camera sometimes shaky, his eyes tired—but it made a difference. And even if he never intended to become a de facto public educator, the moment demanded it. So, he kept filming and posting, bridging the gap between the hospital's frantic pace and people's need for steady reassurance.

Another Comrade Fallen

Without sounding dramatic, I think of our time during the COVID pandemic as a veteran might think of their time served during a war. We saw things that were hard to describe, which you couldn't empathize with unless you were there. We would see patients pass away and then have to go home after our shift and act as if nothing had happened.

David Rossi, a Critical Care Physician Associate in the BayCare Health System, lived the nightmare of the pandemic day after day. The walls of the ICU held the echoes of sobs, the sharp intakes of breath as families were told their loved ones wouldn't be coming home. He watched hands go limp, chests rise and fall for the last time, eyes that once held fear grow empty. He saw ventilators humming, pumping air into bodies that had already given up, offering the illusion of life when there was none left. No matter how many hands his team held, no matter how many desperate efforts they made, the outcome was the same. David wiped the sweat from his forehead, blinked away the sting in his eyes, and braced himself for the next shift, where he knew—without a doubt—he would have to watch more people die.

Like many healthcare providers, David felt the emotional toll of the pandemic. He likened his experiences in critical care to soldiers navigating war—bound by duty, bonded by sacrifice, and surrounded by loss. New emotions rose with each patient that passed. Each patient lost was another comrade fallen; another name etched into the memory of those who fought to keep them alive. And yet, amid the chaos, they had no time to mourn. The war wasn't over.

Hundreds of patients looked to him for help, their eyes pleading for survival, and David had to decide—did he let his emotions surface, or did he bury them for the sake of the next fight?

David was also concerned about those patients who, due to apprehension and unfounded rhetoric, refused to visit hospitals until they were in critical condition. Unfortunately, many of these delayed arrivals led to unfortunate outcomes. Even now, despite the devastating losses and the undeniable toll of the pandemic, misinformation still lingers.

This widespread distrust made it even more critical for healthcare providers to adapt in real-time, ensuring that patients received the care they needed despite the barriers. For David, this meant working in a virtual ICU command center—a groundbreaking approach to critical care that allowed providers to oversee patients remotely with advanced monitoring systems. Each provider had a station with six computer monitors displaying patient progress notes, real-time telemetry, and lab data. With a camera feed, David could look directly into a patient's room, watching ventilator waveforms, medication drip rates, and, most importantly, the patient themselves. With the help of bedside nurses, he could assess their condition in ways that had never before been possible outside the physical ICU. He could watch as respiratory therapists performed intubations, guide sedation protocols, and catch signs of deterioration before they spiraled into crisis.

This wasn't just an evolution in technology—it was an evolution in survival. Virtual critical care meant David could intervene faster, reducing the time between symptoms appearing and action being taken. It allowed overburdened hospitals to manage more patients, keeping ICU beds from overflowing. And for David, it created a layer of protection—physically and emotionally—between him and the constant wave of death he had come to know too well.

David described the practice of virtual critical care as groundbreaking because it allowed for improved healthcare collaboration. This practice not only helped healthcare providers easily connect with others with the push of a button but also shortened the time required to establish a relationship between medical providers and patients, offering a ray of hope during the pandemic as the hospitals continued to fill to capacity.

With developing technologies like telehealth and virtual ICUs, healthcare providers like David felt reassured knowing they could instantly monitor and visualize a patient at any time, leading to more favorable outcomes.

Unwelcome

Imagine working extra days and longer hours with patients from various backgrounds during a pandemic. Now, picture those patients using abusive language toward you as they take out their anger and frustration.

This scenario was the case for many providers like Dr. Vidya Raman, an anesthesiologist, and it led to burnout.

In 2020, Dr. Raman's administrative team laid off workers due to fewer scheduled surgeries. However, a resurgence in anesthesiology cases in 2022 prompted the rehiring of workers. Those laid off were reluctant to return partly because they were scarred by mistreatment from patients and administration. Many people transitioned to other fields with shorter hours, where they felt respected and acknowledged for their contributions. As a result, the healthcare industry faced staff shortages, leading to increased burnout among the remaining healthcare providers.

The patients who come in now are not nice at all. They get violent and use abusive language. After two years of COVID-19, we are not ready to deal with abusive patients. Some people feel entitled and treat us as commodities to vent their frustration. Why can't they see that we are just doing our job?

For Dr. Raman and many of her colleagues, the hostility wasn't limited to the patients—it came from all directions. Hospitals laid off workers in 2020 when elective surgeries plummeted, then scrambled to rehire them when cases surged again in 2022. But many refused to return, weary from the mistreatment they'd endured—not just from administration, but from the very patients they had risked their lives to save. The scars ran deep, and for those who stayed, the strain only worsened. Staffing shortages meant longer shifts, increased patient loads, and no room to recover from the trauma they had absorbed. A 2022 systematic review published in *Frontiers in Psychology* found that nearly 47% of healthcare workers experienced workplace violence during the COVID-19 pandemic. Physicians bore the brunt, with a staggering 68% reporting physical or verbal attacks. Some were screamed at in hallways. Others had objects thrown at them. Many were outright threatened with harm.[12]

And yet, they had no choice but to continue.

When administrators laid off healthcare workers, many perceived it as an opportunity to explore and settle into other fields where they would get paid more, have a reasonable work schedule, and be respected for their efforts.

Even those who chose to stay in healthcare, especially nurses, transitioned into practicing telehealth or became traveling health professionals because the lifestyle was more flexible, and pay was higher. Hospitals' contract labor expenses soared by well over 100% during the pandemic

---

[12] Ramzi ZS, Fatah PW, Dalvandi A. Prevalence of workplace violence against healthcare workers during the COVID-19 pandemic: A systematic review and meta-analysis. *Front Psychol.* 2022 May 29;13:896156. doi: 10.3389/fpsyg.2022.896156.

staffing crisis. One analysis noted that demand for travel RNs jumped 35% in 2020 and another ~40% in 2021.[13]

As a result, many hospitals lost employees. A hospital that needs more employees often cannot generate enough revenue, as additional staffing is required to perform surgeries or supervise hospitals.

The whole healthcare system is shaken and crumbled by COVID-19. 2023 will be a year of reassessing many things in health care, including the need for skilled workers. The situation could be better. I can see more people leaving in the times to come. I worked more during the holiday season because the hospital lacked workers. I was on call on December 26th, 27th, 28th, and 31st. Last year, I barely had one week of vacation.

The system has alienated healthcare workers, overworked them, and failed to see that they are people with personal lives and responsibilities. They are constantly asked to work long hours in high-risk situations without having adequate PPE.

What we went through during the pandemic is not worth the amount of work we do and the mental anguish we went through. On top of that, there is very little gratitude for our work. Most of us are not in healthcare for money but rather for the feeling that we are doing something good for people. We expect to be treated respectfully and not exploited or abused.

---

[13] Odom-Forren J. Travel nursing: price gouging or supply and demand? *J Perianesth Nurs.* 2022 Apr;37(2):153-4. doi: 10.1016/j.jopan.2022.01.013. PMID: 35422269; PMCID: PMC9000908.

During COVID-19, physicians and other healthcare providers dealt with cases of life and death every day. They consoled broken families who worried about the safety of their loved ones. Many were around patients who were very sick and had contagious infections. They were responsible for making families understand what their loved ones were going through. A 2021 study revealed that nearly half of all healthcare workers reported significant burnout symptoms, such as emotional exhaustion and depersonalization, directly impacting their ability to provide high-quality patient care.[14]

Despite this stress, healthcare providers had to make rational and educated decisions that kept the patients' best interests in mind. Even though some families were gracious enough to treat them with respect, many people treated them as commodities that they could use to lessen their frustration.

In the future, the healthcare system must prioritize treating healthcare workers as the invaluable human beings they are. The burnout rates of healthcare providers show an urgent need for systemic changes that support the mental, emotional, and physical well-being of medical professionals. Addressing this issue is not only about improving the lives of healthcare workers but also ensuring the overall effectiveness and sustainability of the healthcare system itself.

To reduce burnout, administrators and policymakers must recognize the vital importance of fair treatment and

---

[14] Cyr S, Marcil MJ, Marin MF, Tardif JC, Guay S, Guertin MC, et al. Factors Associated With Burnout, Post-traumatic Stress and Anxio-Depressive Symptoms in Healthcare Workers 3 Months Into the COVID-19 Pandemic: An Observational Study. Front Psychiatry. 2021 Jul 8;12:668278.

workplace appreciation. They can start by implementing reasonable work schedules that allow for adequate rest and recovery.

One 2023 study showed that nurses who work 12-hour shifts or longer experience increased burnout.[15] Flexible scheduling options and better staffing ratios can alleviate the overwhelming workloads that many healthcare professionals face daily.

Additionally, competitive compensation that reflects the value of skilled labor is essential. Healthcare workers often endure grueling conditions, and fair pay serves as both an acknowledgment of their expertise and a practical means of improving their quality of life.

However, fair schedules and good pay alone will not fully address the problem. Healthcare systems must create environments that foster emotional support. Regular mental health check-ins, access to counseling services, and opportunities for career advancement can empower workers to thrive in their roles. These actions will ensure that healthcare professionals can continue providing compassionate and effective care that patients depend on daily.

---

[15] Dall'Ora C, Ejebu OZ, Ball J, Griffiths P. Shift work characteristics and burnout among nurses: cross-sectional survey. Occupational Medicine. 2023 May 18;73(4):199–204.

Can't Save Everyone

The expectation is to save everyone, and that is not always possible. Sometimes, the patient dies despite all efforts. I do my best to save those that I can, and if I cannot, I strive to help them pass with dignity and companionship.

While prioritizing and saving every patient is ideal, it is often unattainable. Despite the best efforts, some diseases are incurable, and death becomes inevitable. There is only so much healthcare workers can do against COVID-19. The best a healthcare provider can do in untreatable cases is to have a meaningful discussion with the patient about their end-of-life preferences and help them choose to die with dignity. This was the unfortunate reality that Dr. Sommer Aldulaimi, a family physician and co-director of a global health program, was reminded of during the pandemic, especially in this story below.

Dr. Aldulaimi encountered a 73-year-old patient with COVID-19 who required increasing levels of oxygen each day. The patient's condition worsened, so Dr. Aldulaimi informed the patient about the potential need for intubation, a procedure involving the insertion of a tube in her mouth to help her breathe. Given the patient's age and health conditions, she realized that intubation may be risky. The patient's condition continued to worsen, and she was near the end of her life. The patient eventually chose to refuse intubation. Around this time, Dr. Aldulaimi spoke with hospital administration to allow an exception to the visitor policy to allow the patient to see her husband, who was finally granted permission to see her. He was able to spend a final, precious moment with her before she passed away.

I had a conversation with her and her husband. I told them that we had tried everything we could, and now one of our options was to remove her oxygen mask and have both of you be together for one last time. I wanted her to be comfortable and free of pain. Another option was to intubate her, but she would likely still die.

After removing her oxygen mask, the patient passed away within fifteen minutes, with her husband by her side, a rare comfort during the pandemic. Witnessing so many patients die was draining, even for the most emotionally and mentally strong. COVID-19 created a gloomy loneliness about death, with patients often dying without loved ones by their side. Even with healthcare providers present, their protective gear made them appear more like astronauts than humans, alienating patients. Healthcare providers struggled without support also but came together to support their patients and one another.

We were not letting families into the hospital at the beginning of the pandemic. So many people died alone, and I did not want them to die alone, so I would go to their rooms and hold their hand for a few minutes. Sadly, I could not be there the whole time because other patients needed help.

Preparing for the pandemic, the hospital used its offices and call rooms to create an intensive care unit for COVID-19 patients. During the initial days of the pandemic, a COVID-19 team was responsible for admitting patients infected with SARS-CoV-2. Quickly, the team became overwhelmed, leading to the decision to rotate multiple teams weekly. Though adjusting was difficult, the team adapted to the changing situation by supporting each other.

I was in charge of 24 residents who were learning and training. It was my duty to protect those residents as well. All their rotations in outside institutions were canceled as most clinics were closed. We brought all the residents back home and placed them in their hospital. We let them see COVID-19 patients because it was important for their education. We had to preserve our residents' learning while ensuring they were safe. Every day, I felt like I was going into battle to fight the virus and protect my people.

When healthcare workers were overwhelmed with new COVID-19 patients, doctors from different specialties and their teams distributed the workload appropriately, trying to lighten it.

I remember being in the hospital with my colleague, an internal medicine specialist, one night. We would sit in my office and discuss our teams' workloads. I remember an emergency when she was caring for a patient. I ran to her patient's room to help. Later that same night, she helped my resident. We often evaluated patients together to see if they needed to be admitted. We couldn't have survived those nights without each other!

Dr. Aldulaimi stated there was a lot of fear and anxiety related to COVID-19. Healthcare workers were caring for patients with a highly contagious condition they initially knew little about. They had no confirmed answer about how the virus spread and had to ensure the safety of their families and staff while caring for patients. Many healthcare workers did not see their families for months until they got vaccinated, not wanting to expose their loved ones to the virus.

I refused to see my family and husband because I couldn't put their lives in danger. After removing my hospital scrubs in the garage and sanitizing myself, I would go inside the house. My family did not sign up to be healthcare workers, but I did. I wanted to protect my loved ones while also caring for the community. I couldn't run away from it!

I remember canceling festivals, waving at my parents from the car, and dropping gifts outside. After getting the vaccination, I was overwhelmed with happiness and went to see my parents right away. I couldn't control my tears while hugging them. It was unbelievable.

Although healthcare workers tried to protect as many people as possible, they could not be everywhere. Some patients, fearful of COVID-19, refused to come in for regular checkups. Dr. Aldulaimi had an older female patient who refused to come to the clinic due to fear of contracting COVID-19. She regularly talked with the doctor about her health, mentioning occasional fatigue. She attributed it to a lack of social interaction or not going outside often.

After a year, she returned to the clinic and lost a tremendous amount of weight, which she never mentioned over the phone. A CT scan revealed that she had a rare type of cancer that had metastasized, spreading to other parts of her body. Had she come to the clinic earlier, the doctor would have detected the symptoms and started treatment. While staying at home was crucial to avoid exposure, many people lost their lives to other conditions because they couldn't get help in time.

I was affected by her diagnosis. I was disappointed and did feel that I could have detected her condition earlier had I seen her in person. Now, she is in hospice, and she is very sick.

Reflecting on her experiences, Dr. Aldulaimi strived to balance saving every patient and accepting the inevitability of death. These challenges emphasize the need for teamwork and help in successfully treating patients, and the lessons learned will shape a more resilient and empathetic healthcare system.

Supporting Dr. Aldulaimi's narrative, a 2021 article published in the Cureus journal explained how the pandemic created emotional isolation for patients and caregivers, with the inability to offer meaningful communication or emotional support due to personal protective equipment (PPE) and physical distancing measures.[16] The palliative care professionals in the article mention how PPE became a barrier to providing compassionate care, with healthcare workers "appearing like astronauts" rather than humans. Dr. Aldulaimi's practice of holding patients' hands or staying with them for a while before they passed away mirrors the efforts mentioned in the article to overcome these communication barriers and provide emotional comfort.

---

[16] Tavares P, Rodrigues C, Neto IG. The Impact of COVID-19 on Palliative Care: Perspective of Healthcare Professionals. Cureus. 2021 Nov;13(11):e19522.

The ethical dilemmas presented by COVID-19, particularly the decisions around who should receive intensive care or who should be intubated, are also discussed in both Dr. Aldulaimi's story and the article. The palliative care professionals in the study wrestled with difficult choices, like balancing life-saving interventions with the patient's wishes and quality of life. Dr. Aldulaimi faced similar challenges when informing her patient about the possible need for intubation, knowing that, in her case, it may only prolong suffering. Healthcare providers must continue to uphold the principles of beneficence and justice, especially in situations where healthcare resources are limited and decisions have to be made quickly. In Dr. Aldulaimi's case, the decision to respect the patient's wishes and allow her to pass with dignity rather than pushing for intubation highlights the application of these ethical principles.

Masked Emotions

Two years into the pandemic, the idea of normal suddenly changed. Daily commutes to work and trips to restaurants and grocery stores carried the worry of contracting a virus, and visiting loved ones required preparation like never before. Although some professions allowed remote options, many medical professionals worked in high-risk environments, including anaesthesiologists like Dr. John Crowe, whose role was to assess and ensure patient care and safety before, during, and after surgical procedures at the UC Health Hospital. Dr. Crowe witnessed firsthand the devastating impact of the virus, even on otherwise healthy individuals. He recalls one particular case that underscored the virus's unpredictability:

I had a patient who was the CEO of a company, and she contracted the virus before vaccines were available. She was a young lady in excellent health, but the virus affected her to the extent that she could barely walk. While walking to the kitchen, she fell and hit her jaw against the table, breaking it. She lay there for hours on the floor until she could get to the phone and call for help.

Although many believed that COVID-19 only affected elderly individuals, particularly those with pre-existing conditions, the world saw seemingly healthy individuals become ill due to the coronavirus. The virus did not differentiate by age, as we saw the young, fit, and healthy getting sick. Along with getting sick, some individuals did not have others for support or help.

As Dr. Crowe treated these patients, he found it challenging to stay present for the entire recovery process because others needed his medical expertise. Nonetheless, he tried his best to support his patients with meaningful conversations, which were often emotionally charged, especially when afflicted patients did not have the reassuring presence of their loved ones due to safety measures.

If we want to understand a fraction of what COVID-19 patients were feeling, we could put ourselves in a patient's shoes. We may imagine sitting in a hospital room filled with hushed whispers, palpable tension, and masked faces and hearing a daunting medical diagnosis. The absence of familiar faces and comforting touch may worry us and have us navigate our fears and anxieties alone.

Moreover, Dr. Crowe and other providers felt emotionally disconnected from their patients because they could not see each other's facial expressions and found it difficult to console them.

I could see that the lady's eyes were full of fear and worry, and I was wearing a surgical face mask while talking to her, and it felt like a barrier in our interaction.

Despite these limitations, Dr. Crowe committed to ensuring his patients felt heard and could express their thoughts openly. Physicians and patients rely on face-to-face interactions to communicate empathy, understanding, and other caring signals.

I remember one particular case. The surgeon had just placed a tracheostomy tube into the patient's neck, and the patient was losing oxygen. I immediately thought the ventilator was not providing enough flow or there was a leak somewhere. Fortunately, I planned for this type of situation. I grabbed a manual breathing bag, filled it with 100 percent oxygen, plugged it in, turned up the flow, and hand-ventilated the patient, bringing them up to higher oxygen saturation. I was able to troubleshoot where the leak was, and we could transition back to the ventilator. It was a terrifying scenario, but we brought it under control.

Dr. Crowe described how, while treating patients, the use of PPE created a barrier between him and his patients, which made it difficult to communicate empathy and offer the emotional support that many patients needed during their isolation. His example of the CEO patient, with her eyes full of fear while Dr. Crowe spoke to her through a surgical mask, underscores the emotional disconnect created by the physical limitations of PPE. A 2020 systematic review identifies that mental health issues such as anxiety, depression, and insomnia were widespread among healthcare workers.[17] One contributing factor to these issues was the isolation and disconnection experienced by healthcare workers due to both physical distancing measures and the mental strain of working in high-pressure, high-risk environments.

Both Dr. Crowe's personal experience and the study findings highlight the emotional burden placed on healthcare workers during the pandemic. Dr. Crowe's struggle to

---

[17] Pappa S, Ntella V, Giannakas T, Giannakoulis VG, Papoutsi E, Katsaounou P. Prevalence of depression, anxiety, and insomnia among healthcare workers during the COVID-19 pandemic: A systematic review and meta-analysis. Brain, Behavior, and Immunity. 2020 Aug;88:901–7.

emotionally connect with patients while dealing with the fear and anxiety of patients isolated from their families mirrors the mental health impact identified in the review, which found that healthcare workers experienced increased anxiety and depression due to their roles during the crisis.

Log In, Check Up

Hina Mazharuddin had always been ahead of the curve. A Physician Associate (PA) with over 15 years of experience, she transitioned into virtual care in 2018—long before telemedicine became a necessity rather than an option. Specializing in obesity medicine and urgent care, she saw the potential of telehealth not as a replacement for in-person visits but as a tool to bridge gaps in accessibility. Patients with chronic conditions, those in rural communities, or individuals struggling with transportation could now receive consistent, high-quality care without the usual barriers.

Her early commitment to telemedicine wasn't just about convenience; it was about ensuring patients had access to the care they needed when they needed it. This vision led her to take on leadership roles beyond her clinical work. As vice president of Physician Assistants in Virtual Medicine and Telemedicine (PAVMT), an AAPA-affiliated organization dedicated to expanding PA representation in telehealth, she took charge of education initiatives, training future providers in the nuances of virtual care.

By the time COVID-19 upended healthcare systems worldwide, Hina was already fluent in telemedicine. While others scrambled to adapt, she was guiding her colleagues, integrating artificial intelligence in patient monitoring, and ensuring telehealth was more than just a stopgap solution. Her journey into virtual care was never a reaction to the pandemic—it was a deliberate choice, driven by a deep understanding that medicine had to evolve to meet patients where they were, long before the world realized just how crucial that would become.

Additionally, the members involved in PAVMT also give advice, networking, resources, and research to improve telemedicine for PAs and PA students. They have a range of blog posts, webinars, certification series, and other resources developed by experienced PAs. These resources include articles on partnering with a physician in virtual practice, understanding how Medicare and Medicaid operate within telehealth, staying updated on billing and coding, and navigating telehealth.

Moving from the benefits of the new group towards telemedicine, the pandemic's challenges pushed healthcare teams to adopt innovative solutions that were difficult to implement and teach. One of the most significant changes was the rapid integration of telemedicine into hospitals and clinics.

While telemedicine was not successful in every situation, Hina Mazharuddin proactively trained her staff to become "telemedicine champions." She helped educate them on how to use the platform, give consent, gather vitals using at-home resources, and more.

Initially, the virtual urgent care I worked at faced challenges during the pandemic due to its setup. The original model featured a kiosk inside a grocery store, where patients would arrive and be greeted by a medical assistant (MA). The MA would then connect with me via a virtual platform to provide care, acting as my hands while I was miles away. However, with social distancing and restrictions, we had to adapt quickly, discovering new ways to connect with patients and ensure safety for everyone involved.

As telemedicine advanced, its reach expanded beyond urgent care, opening doors for preventive screenings and chronic disease management.

Early detection of diabetic retinopathy is crucial.

Diabetic retinopathy is a complication of diabetes that affects the eyes, caused by damage to the blood vessels in the retina. Over time, high blood sugar levels can weaken these vessels, leading to leakage, swelling, and even abnormal growth of new blood vessels, which can result in vision loss or blindness if left untreated.

Early detection of diabetic retinopathy is crucial because symptoms often don't appear until significant damage has already occurred.

With the help of telemedicine and AI, we can extend our screening to a broader population. We use an autonomous AI machine that captures images of a patient's retina and generates an initial reading. This reading is sent to me, and I then schedule a telemedicine visit with the patient to review the results. If necessary, I refer them to a specialist for further evaluation and treatment.

Telemedicine allowed providers like Hina to see more patients than they would typically see in person. It offered greater flexibility, allowing appointments to fit easily into patients' schedules, including during work hours. It saved patients' time and eliminated the need to travel to the clinic.

Now, they had the option to avoid taking off from work, arranging transportation, paying for parking, or finding childcare to see a provider. There were still some problems, but it made life more convenient for patients.

Muntaha, a vital team member involved in producing this book, has seen how individuals from low socioeconomic backgrounds find it hard to seek healthcare. Working as a research intern at the University of Florida's Institute of Aging, Muntaha speaks with research participants over age 65 regarding their participation in research studies about geriatric medicine. She observed that many participants canceled appointments due to rising gas prices. Telemedicine appointments allow participants to get free health checkups, a chance to get hundreds of dollars of compensation, and evidence-based supplements beneficial for health.

The cost of gas kept climbing. Groceries, rent—everything more expensive than the year before. For some, the choice was clear: skip the appointment. Save the money. Hope for the best.

But telemedicine changed that. It cut the cost of care—not in doctor's fees, but in the hidden price of getting there. No long drives, no missed work shifts, no need to weigh a co-pay against a tank of gas. It also made asking for help easier. A nagging symptom didn't have to turn into an emergency before a patient reached out. They could check in early, before the problem got worse.

When patients have medical needs, it isn't always easy for them to visit the clinic. Telehealth allows patients to connect with me from home with just the push of a button. This saves time for both patients and medical providers.

Recognizing your limitations is also important. Not all conditions are suitable to manage via telemedicine. It's important to triage patients to a higher level of care when necessary to make sure they receive the appropriate medical attention.

Telemedicine is a tool to eliminate inconveniences. If telemedicine is not enough to treat the patient, healthcare providers must refer them to a facility that can provide better care.

In telemedicine, being resourceful and approaching challenges creatively can be very beneficial. For instance, if a patient contacts me during a synchronous audio-visual telemedicine visit with a rash on their arm, I may need to determine whether the rash blanches. This can help differentiate between conditions like hives (an allergic reaction) versus purpura (purple spots under the skin). While it might seem straightforward to ask the patient to press on the rash and describe whether it blanches, medical training emphasizes the importance of objective findings on physical examination over subjective reports.

To address this, I might ask the patient to use a common household item, such as a clear tumbler glass, to press against the rash while holding it up to the camera. This way, I can observe directly whether the rash blanches or not. This approach is not unique to telemedicine; it's akin to the Glass test or Tumbler test used for identifying meningitis rashes. By thinking creatively, we can obtain the necessary information.

Telemedicine can provide valuable data by using the resources that patients already have at home, such as thermometers, weighing scales, and sometimes even blood pressure cuffs, pulse oximeters, smartwatches, or rings. Even using something as simple as ice can be a practical method for assessing temperature sensation.

Seeing all of the benefits of telemedicine, Hina's practice continues to work to implement virtual and in-person visits. For conditions Hina can manage through telemedicine, she offers virtual consultations, providing patients with a flexible option. For those who require or prefer in-person care, her office ensures a safe environment by adhering to strict COVID-19 protocols, including vaccinations and masking, minimizing waiting room exposure through vehicle waiting options, and limiting the number of people in the clinic. This model allows patients to remain connected with their healthcare providers while receiving the care they need, whether virtually or in person.

Although implementing telehealth was not the easiest, it allowed providers and patients to collaborate conveniently during the pandemic by addressing new problems and limiting the spread of COVID-19.

Click. Type. Bill. Repeat.

When the pandemic started, I realized that the insurance healthcare system was not as worried about patients as I expected. It was more worried about how many patients we could bill every day for different diagnoses. Many patients are in insurance programs that do not cover their medical tests, and they cannot afford the tests.

Frustrated by watching her patients' health suffer due to these limitations, Dr. Deepti Mundkur made a bold decision—she left her insurance-based clinic and founded *My Happy Doctor*, a practice dedicated to direct primary care and affordable healthcare.

With this practice, her goal was to provide direct primary care by spending more time with her patients. Unlike traditional practices, she used telemedicine and longer house calls to build meaningful patient relationships.

In her previous job, Dr. Mundkur often felt rushed, with limited time to spend with each patient. A 2021 study shows that an average primary care exam is about 18 minutes.[18] She sat across from her patient, trying to focus on their concerns, but her mind was already pulled in a dozen directions. The knock on the door would come soon—always too soon. A medical assistant, clipboard in hand, would peek in: "Next patient is ready." It wasn't a request; it was a reminder to wrap things up.

---

[18] Neprash HT, Everhart A, McAlpine D, Smith LB, Sheridan B, Cross DA. Measuring primary care exam length using electronic health record data. *Med Care*. 2021 Jan;59(1):62-66. doi: 10.1097/MLR.0000000000001450. PMID: 33301282.

She'd nod, force a polite smile, and turn back to the patient in front of her, but the rhythm of the clinic didn't allow for pauses. Document this, prescribe that, click, type, move on. Behind her, the electronic health record (EHR) system blinked relentlessly, demanding updates.

It wasn't just the interruptions. It was the relentless paperwork, the endless charting, the insurance codes that dictated care more than medical judgment.

Doctors spend twice as much time on paperwork as they do with patients.[19] Click. A symptom recorded. Click. A diagnosis entered. Click. A justification added—not just for medical accuracy, but to satisfy insurance requirements. Miss a code, forget a modifier, and reimbursement stalls. The claim gets rejected. The appeal drags on. A treatment that made perfect sense in the exam room suddenly doesn't fit the billing guidelines.

The work doesn't end when the last patient walks out the door. Long after the clinic lights dim, doctors sit hunched over their screens, navigating electronic health records that weren't designed for them. Drop-down menus. Endless clicks. Notes structured not around patient care, but around what insurance will approve. The shift to value-based care only deepens the burden. It's not enough to document what they did—they have to prove why it meets a metric, why it checks the right boxes, why it deserves payment. The rules aren't made by doctors. But they have to follow them anyway.

---

[19] Neprash HT, Everhart A, McAlpine D, Smith LB, Sheridan B, Cross DA. Measuring primary care exam length using electronic health record data. *Med Care*. 2021 Jan;59(1):62-66. doi: 10.1097/MLR.0000000000001450. PMID: 33301282.

To Dr. Mundkur, it was the feeling that medicine—the kind where you actually listen, where you understand a patient's life beyond their symptoms—was slipping further away.

She left work drained, not because she had cared for too many patients, but because she hadn't been able to care for them the way she wanted.

Dr. Mundkur focused on her new practice during the pandemic, and she was grateful to see it grow. She saw the positive changes it brought to her work-life balance, such as allowing her to work from home with her husband and puppies instead of spending long hours in the clinic. In this practice, she made house calls to her patients and saw their homes, families, and all sorts of prized possessions. This gave her a deeper understanding of her patients beyond their illnesses.

During house calls, I saw a different perspective of patients that I would have never been able to see in a clinic setting. They showed me their grandchildren and chickens in the backyard. It was as if time stood still when I was with my patients. It helped me develop a more personal relationship with my patients.

One significant aspect that Dr. Mundkur implemented in her practice was her approach to discussing the COVID-19 vaccine with her patients. She spoke with a patient who had recovered from COVID-19 and was apprehensive about getting vaccinated. The patient read about the vaccine from various sources and was unsure about its safety, so Dr. Mundkur provided evidence-based facts without pushing her beliefs, allowing the patient to make an informed decision.

I did not approach the conversation trying to change her mind. I gave her the facts and let her make her own decision. I have seen the strong impact vaccines have on communities. I am pro-vaccine, but I also know there are side effects with any medicine. It's about evaluating the pros and cons and informing patients so they can decide.

She chose the vaccine. Then she did more than that—she started encouraging others. Colleagues. Friends. Family. The same patient who had once hesitated now stood tall, telling people why she had made her decision.

At her practice, she did things differently. She spent time, real time, with patients. Asked about their pets, their families, their lives outside of their charts. She made space for them in a way she hadn't been able to before, and they felt it. The practice grew.

Dr. Mundkur's clinic, *My Happy Doctor*, evolved into more than just a medical practice. It became a place where patients felt seen. A lifeline for people in remote towns, connected not by a waiting room but by a screen. Through telemedicine, she built relationships with patients she had never met in person, earning their trust one conversation at a time.

I have developed excellent relationships with patients who live in remote parts of California, where there are fewer doctors than in other areas. Telemedicine is the best option, given the circumstances. It's amazing that I can be exactly who I would be in a house call, except I'm sitting in my home.

After going through the experience of working long hours on endless paperwork taking away time from real patient care, Dr. Mundkur built a practice during the pandemic, a practice that prioritized patient care over billing. Her practice demonstrated that telemedicine could provide quality healthcare while allowing physicians to connect with their patients meaningfully. Through her positive attitude and dedication, Dr. Mundkur showed that it's possible to transform patient care even in challenging times.

Summary and Reflection

Each account, charged with quiet desperation and understated heroism, reveals not only individual endurance but also the profound structural shortcomings that allowed the pandemic to carve so deeply into our society. What can we learn from these frontline experiences, and how must our policies and ethics evolve to prevent such a crisis from devastating us again?

The sudden necessity of telemedicine revealed a paradox: it offered unprecedented access to healthcare, especially in remote rural areas where isolation previously meant neglect. Yet, beneath the optimism and technological promise lay uncomfortable truths. While telehealth could alleviate disparities, does it risk reinforcing them if policymakers fail to ensure equitable digital access? Telemedicine must supplement, never fully replace, physical care; otherwise, we risk deepening divides rather than bridging them.

The crisis also cast an unforgiving light on healthcare worker burnout, not as a novel challenge, but as a chronic condition exacerbated to a breaking point. Dr. Atkinson's morning huddles offered brief relief, moments of solidarity amidst chaos, but they also raised larger questions. Why must healthcare workers constantly shoulder unbearable burdens before institutions acknowledge their mental health needs? Are we satisfied to merely provide emotional support, or must we confront and rectify the deeper systemic failures—understaffing, inadequate compensation, and unrealistic workloads—that foster burnout in the first place?

Ethical dilemmas during the pandemic were unyielding, forcing healthcare workers into impossible choices: who receives scarce resources, and who must go without? Policies often lagged behind reality, leaving frontline staff isolated, burdened not just by physical exhaustion but by moral injury. Is our healthcare system morally prepared for future crises, and are current guidelines sufficient to guide professionals ethically when resources run thin? We must develop policies grounded not just in logistics, but in compassion, dignity, and fairness.

Innovations such as virtual ICUs demonstrated extraordinary adaptability, rapidly transforming patient care through technology. Yet we must also ask: will this digital revolution privilege efficiency over empathy, distance over connection? Is technological advancement genuinely inclusive, or does it risk commodifying care, further alienating vulnerable populations who may already mistrust medical institutions?

Ultimately, these stories compel us to confront deeper truths about our healthcare system and our society. COVID-19 revealed that resilience is not just an individual trait—it must be built into our systems. We must commit ourselves to understanding not only what happened but why—and more importantly, who bears the cost when systems fail. Our path forward requires courage, honesty, and sustained policy change. Only then can we honor the sacrifices made during the pandemic by building a healthcare system that is equitable, humane, and resilient enough to withstand whatever comes next.

Discussion Questions

1. In what ways did the rapid adoption of telemedicine both mitigate and exacerbate preexisting inequities in healthcare access, and what policy changes could ensure that digital care becomes a bridge rather than a barrier for underserved communities?

2. How can healthcare institutions better support frontline workers to prevent burnout and address the profound emotional toll revealed by experiences like those of Dr. Atkinson and Dr. Goodcoff?

3. What ethical frameworks or guidelines should be developed to help healthcare providers navigate the difficult resource allocation decisions and moral dilemmas that arose during the pandemic?

4. How can the stories of personal sacrifice and systemic failures shared by healthcare professionals inform future reforms to strengthen the resilience and sustainability of our healthcare infrastructure?

5. With technology rapidly transforming patient care—such as through virtual ICUs and telehealth—what strategies can be implemented to ensure that efficiency does not come at the expense of genuine human connection and compassionate care?

Part 2: Mental Health in the Pandemic

Addressing the Psychological Toll

Introduction

Mental health has always mattered, yet for too long it remained hidden, buried beneath stigma and silence. Then came COVID-19, and what was hidden burst into plain sight, revealing how fragile our safety nets truly were. The pandemic didn't create our mental health crisis—it exposed it, laid it bare for everyone to see. In the following chapters, you will hear from those who lived through this upheaval: patients who struggled to find help, providers stretched beyond their limits, and communities grappling with the consequences.

We start by looking at stigma, that powerful force that keeps people from seeking the care they desperately need. Even as mental health became a headline topic, many still hesitated, weighed down by shame, misunderstanding, or fear of judgment. These barriers were not random but deeply woven into the fabric of our culture, fueling cycles of silence and despair.

Then there's isolation. The abrupt loss of everyday routines and social connections didn't just disrupt lives—it shattered them. Students who once thrived found themselves sinking into anxiety; healthcare workers, hailed as heroes, privately struggled with trauma and burnout; individuals already fighting invisible battles watched helplessly as their support systems crumbled.

This distress did not happen in isolation; it fueled another crisis—substance abuse. As people reached for anything to numb the pain, alcohol and drug use soared, creating a parallel emergency that overwhelmed already strained healthcare systems. The ripple effects touched everyone, from exhausted emergency room staff to families desperately seeking support that wasn't there.

Yet amid this chaos, a transformation began. Telemedicine exploded overnight, reshaping the landscape of mental health care. Virtual sessions offered lifelines, bridging gaps created by lockdowns and fear. The COVID-19 pandemic acted as a catalyst for the rapid expansion of telehealth services, including online therapy platforms like BetterHelp. This surge in demand led to substantial growth in BetterHelp's user base and revenue. In 2020, BetterHelp earned over $345 million in revenue, which more than doubled to over $720 million in 2021. In 2022, BetterHelp's revenue continued to grow, surpassing $1 billion.[20] But this shift wasn't without its complications. Digital care exposed deep inequities—access barriers, privacy concerns, and the reality that screens couldn't always replace genuine human connection, especially for those facing severe psychological distress.

Throughout these chapters, you'll hear directly from people who bore the brunt of these challenges: psychologists fighting burnout, patients navigating virtual care, and frontline workers holding communities together by threads. Their stories make clear one unavoidable truth: mental health intersects every part of our lives—education, work, healthcare, family—and addressing it effectively demands more than temporary fixes. It requires profound cultural shifts, real policy changes, and a commitment to seeing

---

[20] Federal Trade Commission. BetterHelp Complaint Final. 2023. Available from: https://www.ftc.gov/system/files/ftc_gov/pdf/2023169betterhelpcomplaintfinal.pdf

mental health not as an isolated issue, but as a fundamental part of our shared humanity.

As you read, consider not just the struggles depicted here, but also the possibilities for change. Mental health impacts us all, whether we acknowledge it or not. To confront this reality is to take a crucial step toward a society that refuses to leave anyone behind.

When Classrooms Went Dark

Dr. Renee Causey-Upton, an occupational therapy professor at Eastern Kentucky University (EKU), recognized the increasing anxiety levels among her occupational therapy students during the COVID-19 pandemic. Even before the pandemic, this generation of students had the highest rates of mental health conditions compared to previous generations. The reasons were layered—rising academic pressures, the influence of social media, and an increasing awareness and diagnosis of mental health disorders. Then came the pandemic. The added anxiety was likely due to the lockdowns and university closures, which disrupted their routines and stripped away their normalcy. Their structured schedules with classes, exams, social interactions, and recreational activities were gone.

Before the pandemic, the certainty of a daily schedule, including classes and sports activities, helped students stay focused. Routine creates stability, helping students manage their time, stay engaged, and maintain a sense of progress. Knowing what came next reduced decision fatigue and minimized distractions, allowing them to focus on their studies. When their schools were shut down, their plans were thrown into disarray, and the uncertainty about what lay ahead only added to their anxiety levels.

Imagine being a student already juggling school-related stress, trying to stay on track for graduation and a job. Then, without warning, everything that kept you grounded—

classes, study groups, the rhythm of campus life—is gone. Each canceled class, each day spent staring at a screen instead of sitting in a lecture hall, makes it harder to feel like you're moving forward. You no longer have the friendly check-ins with classmates who understood exactly what you were going through, the small nods of encouragement, the quiet laughs over a tough assignment. Those little moments—ones that made the stress feel manageable—disappear, and with them, the sense of progress and connection. The path that once felt clear is now uncertain, and with every passing day, the fear creeps in—what if everything you've worked for just slips away?

Dr. Causey-Upton shared that most programs, including hers, tried accommodating students' needs, but access to specific resources, such as student organizations that promoted camaraderie and connectedness, decreased. While counseling services, technological support, academic support and other services dd become available virtually, students nevertheless still experienced social disconnection. The shutdown of universities worldwide created a new epidemic of separation and isolation alongside the virus.

For some students, university life was not just about education but also an escape from emotional, mental, and financial turmoil at home. A simple coffee break or lunch with a friend could provide a much-needed distraction from family problems. Because the pandemic severely limited social interactions, students were forced to remain at home, where isolation and a lack of outside support often intensified family tensions, strained relationships, and heightened emotional stress. But for some, it did the opposite—it pulled families closer. With school and work no longer dictating their every move, parents and children found themselves sitting at the same table more often, talking, laughing, or just existing in the same space in a way they hadn't before. The forced stillness created room for connection, a kind of closeness that had been lost in the rush of everyday life. As Dr. Causey-Upton put it: "In contrast, the pandemic also served as a way to help family members grow closer and spend time together, which they could not do during school and work." While the pandemic did create opportunities for students to connect more with their family, it also led to learning barriers as well. She stated:

A lot of our students lived in dorms. Due to the pandemic, they had to return home and live with their families, which was a tough transition for them.

Many of these students worked from home while also having their family members do their jobs and work remotely. Some students had to sit in restaurant parking lots to attend class virtually because they did not have an adequate internet connection at home.

For students in occupational therapy and other healthcare programs, where direct patient interaction is essential, the loss was more than an inconvenience; it was a roadblock.

Without fieldwork, graduation dates were pushed back. Career paths grew uncertain. Some questioned whether they could even enter the profession they had spent years preparing for. The skills they were supposed to master—helping patients regain independence with their daily occupations and activities, guiding individuals through rehabilitation—felt abstract when confined to a computer screen. Watching demonstrations or reading case studies could never fully replace the experience of working directly with patients.

But the problem wasn't just about delays—it was about access. Many students didn't have the resources to keep up with online learning. Reliable Wi-Fi, quiet study spaces, and access to necessary materials were far from guaranteed. Those from lower-income backgrounds, who relied on campus libraries, study groups, or in-person support, were at an even greater disadvantage. For them, online education wasn't just difficult—it was often unmanageable.

The lack of hands-on training also led to an increase in attrition rates, particularly in healthcare and technical fields where in-person experience is crucial. Some students, discouraged by uncertainty and the growing gap between education and real-world practice, dropped out altogether. Others delayed their studies, waiting for a return to normal that took longer than expected. The pandemic didn't just pause education—it reshaped who could continue and who was left behind.

For those who stuck it out, returning to fieldwork after months—or even years (for those who took an extended break from their studies)—away from hands-on practice was another hurdle. Skills deteriorated without use, and confidence can wane. Some students feared they weren't prepared, questioning whether they had learned enough from remote instruction to handle real-world challenges.

Education was supposed to be the pathway forward, the bridge to stability and opportunity. But for many students, especially those in hands-on fields, the pandemic turned it into an obstacle course—one that some wouldn't make it through.

The system needed them, yet it held them back. Hospitals were desperate—beds filled, staff pushed past their limits, a workforce stretched so thin it was beginning to snap. And yet, the very students training to join them—the ones who had spent years preparing for this moment—were stuck.

No fieldwork, no graduation. No graduation, no job. That's how it felt. Like an unspoken rule, a hard stop. Occupational therapy students, and so many others in healthcare, watched their futures stall overnight. Field placements were canceled, hands-on training shut down, and suddenly, the path they had spent years walking was blocked.

While the country cried out for more healthcare workers, these students sat at home, unable to move forward, trapped in a system that needed them but wouldn't let them in. The irony was suffocating: a healthcare crisis starving for professionals, yet the very ones who had signed up to serve were left waiting, frozen in place.

Grief doesn't wait for a convenient time. It doesn't pause for deadlines, exams, or Zoom meetings. But for many students during the pandemic, there was no space to mourn, no time to process. Loss became something to push through, to manage in between assignments and lectures, as if the weight of a dying loved one could be compartmentalized. Additionally, students losing family members to COVID-19 faced challenges in their academic journeys. They found it difficult to focus, especially when a loved one was suffering or passed away. One example from Dr. Causey-Upton displays some of the challenges students faced with family illness during the pandemic.

A student of mine came to our meeting very upset. After a few minutes, I found out that my student had a family member who contracted COVID-19 and was about to be placed on the ventilator. I asked her why she came given her circumstances. I told her not to worry about the meeting as it could be done at any other time.

This account illustrates how some of the most awful experiences became so normal that students felt they had no choice but to push through their trials. They pushed through while sitting in front of computer screens, surrounded by distractions and fears, with minimal social interaction. They battled traumas, the loss of loved ones, and more. COVID-19 forced many to believe that their traumas were normal and could be neglected in favor of focusing on their academics.

The loss of fieldwork opportunities, especially in fields like occupational therapy, was a significant source of stress for students. Professional opportunities such as internships were halted, creating uncertainty around graduation timelines and career prospects. As Dr. Causey-Upton observed, many programs (including occupational therapy) had to adapt quickly, shifting from in-person classes to virtual platforms due to pandemic restrictions. The transition led to issues like lack of hands-on experience and delays in clinical placements, which was a source of stress for students. A 2023 study in *Frontiers in Medicine* reinforces the idea that virtual learning, while necessary, could not fully replace the experiential and face-to-face aspects of healthcare training.[21] In the study, both students and instructors faced steep learning curves with the new platforms. The study found that beyond technological barriers, the absence of non-verbal communication and the inability to develop essential clinical skills made remote instruction an inadequate substitute for in-person learning. Without direct patient interaction, students were left with gaps in their training, raising concerns about their preparedness for professional practice. The paper mentions that students and teachers alike experienced challenges like insufficient technological infrastructure, lack of non-verbal communication, and the inability to develop clinical skills.

The COVID-19 pandemic exposed a fundamental truth: learning isn't just about absorbing information—it's about doing the work. For students in healthcare programs, the shift to remote learning meant missing out on the very experiences that prepared them for real-world practice. They studied procedures without performing them, analyzed case studies without interacting with patients, and navigated healthcare fields that demand presence from behind a screen. It's clear that fully virtual platforms pose challenges for fields requiring hands-on experience.

The COVID-19 pandemic showed us that we need adaptable learning solutions that preserve essential in-person training, even in times of crisis. Moving forward,

---

[21] Sahu PK, Dalçik H. Editorial: Impact of COVID-19 on healthcare professions education. Front Med. 2023 Aug 7;10:1265811.

institutions, educators, and policymakers must collaborate to develop hybrid models that integrate technology with real-world practice. By ensuring that students can continue gaining field experience, we can maintain the quality of education and workforce readiness, regardless of global disruptions.

The Unclaimed Coffee Mug

Dr. Kawehi Au is a mother, mentor, pediatric hospitalist, caretaker, and, most importantly, a human being.

Her COVID-19 experience represents every healthcare worker's struggle to fulfill their selfless duties while facing the challenges of the pandemic.

Dr. Au described the pandemic not as a blur of headlines and case numbers, but as a daily fight for survival. Each morning, she got up knowing that stepping into the hospital meant gambling with her own life. There was no certainty, no guarantees—just the slow, creeping fear that today could be the day she didn't make it home. She would watch colleagues walk through the same doors, put on the same protective gear, exchange the same weary glances, only for some of them to never return. The empty locker, the unclaimed coffee mug, the name suddenly missing from the shift schedule—each loss chipped away at the illusion that she could somehow make it through untouched. And when it wasn't death, it was the brutal exhaustion, the endless hours, the feeling of being swallowed whole by a system that needed more than it could give.

The pandemic didn't just change her—it forced her to see life through a different lens, one where every moment felt borrowed and every breath a quiet victory. Out of over 6 million lab-confirmed COVID-19 cases reported between

January 1, 2020, and October 12, 2021, approximately 440,044 were healthcare workers, and 1,469 died.[22]

As a single parent, Dr. Au faced an impossible choice each morning: stay home and risk losing the job that kept food on the table or go to work and gamble with her daughter's safety. There was no right answer, only the math of risk and necessity. The thought of bringing the virus home sat in her stomach like a stone, heavy and unmoving. She kept her distance, spoke to her daughter from the other side of the room, a mother shrinking from the very child she longed to hold. Her elderly parents, once a safety net, became another source of fear.

The hospital was its own battlefield—understaffed, chaotic, demanding. But it was home that felt like a war zone. Childcare options vanished overnight. Schools closed. Friends who might have helped were also drowning in their own crises. Every plan she had for balancing motherhood and medicine crumbled, replaced by an exhausting improvisation. Some nights, she came home too drained to do much. The pandemic didn't just stretch her thin—it dismantled the careful systems she had built, leaving her to piece together a life that no longer fit.

As a single mother and healthcare worker, finding childcare during the pandemic became very tricky. At one point, my daughter had to be quarantined because her father contracted COVID-19, and I had just switched jobs. It was

[22] Lin S, Deng X, Ryan I, Zhang K, Zhang W, Oghaghare E, et al. COVID-19 Symptoms and Deaths among Healthcare Workers, United States. Emerg Infect Dis. 2022 Aug;28(8):1624–41.

hard to quarantine her at home while I was at work, and I had no personal time off to take care of her. I also had an older parent who lived with me who was at high risk.

Although Dr. Au's support system has been helpful, many healthcare workers needed help finding similar support for their families. According to the Organization for Economic Co-operation and Development (OECD) data, the U.S. is the only country within the OECD that fails to provide a "statutory entitlement to paid leave on a national basis."[23] In other words, the U.S. does not guarantee paid parental leave, unlike other countries within the OECD.

Countries like Austria, South Korea, Germany, Singapore, and Canada have public health policies that include high-quality childcare programs and government support to keep programs open during the pandemic. The unsustainable support in the U.S. stresses healthcare workers and emphasizes the lack of effective childcare policies.

Adding to the upheaval, Dr. Au moved from the hospital to a clinic, trading urgency for uncertainty. The hospital had been chaos—alarms blaring, patients crashing, decisions made in seconds. The clinic was slower, quieter, its empty slots a reminder that patients were too afraid to come. Each morning, she checked the schedule, dreading more cancellations. The administration wasn't sure the clinic would survive. Then two clinicians were pulled entirely—

[23] OECD (Organisation for Economic Co-operation and Development). PF2.1 Key characteristics of parental leave systems [Internet]. Available from: https://webfs.oecd.org/Els-com/Family_Database/PF2_1_Parental_leave_systems.pdf

sent to swab patients. It was a warning. The real fight was elsewhere, and she feared she might soon be expendable.

Then came another challenge—one she hadn't expected. The clinic served college students, young and restless. Unlike the gasping patients she had treated in the hospital, these students walked in healthy, unbothered. She recalled the videos she saw students partying without masks. At first, frustration burned through her—didn't they see what she had seen? The intubated patients, the families sobbing over video calls, the ones who never made it home?

But anger only exhausted her. She couldn't argue with every skeptic. So, she did what she could. She listened. She met their resistance with calm, their denial with facts. She explained, re-explained, knowing most would brush her off the moment they left. Still, she tried. Not because she expected to change them all, but because she owed it to the ones who might listen. The ones who might think twice before walking into a crowded party, who might keep their masks on a little longer. She couldn't force them to care. But she could still do her job.

I work at a college now, and many students aren't following guidelines. We saw videos of them having parties without masks. It was frustrating, and I started feeling depressed driving to work, thinking that I couldn't believe this was my life.

One day, I asked my boss if he ever felt depressed coming to work. He told me he did not and expressed gratitude. His positive attitude was contagious.

Despite these challenges, the Hippocratic Oath remained Dr. Au's guiding principle. She was a healing hand to everyone, regardless of their perspective on the pandemic. While people ignored guidelines, gathering in crowds and feeling untouchable, Dr. Au watched people she knew—friends, colleagues, mentors—die. They were overworked, exposed, and carrying the weight of a crisis that refused to spare them.

I had a friend, Rufino, a respiratory therapist I had known for years. He lost his life to COVID last year. Then there was Rufino. Back in Guatemala, he had been a doctor, but after coming to the U.S., he retrained as a respiratory therapist. He had a gentle way with patients, making sure mothers could hold their babies, caring for infants on ventilators, even cradling and playing with them when he could. Losing him to something preventable was devastating. We lost a nurse, too. Another ER nurse spent months on life support before being flown to Florida for a lung transplant. It's painful to watch healthcare workers give everything, only for people to still think COVID-19 is a hoax.

Dr. Au never gave up, even when exhaustion settled deep in her bones, even when support and reassurance felt out of reach. Fatigue threatened to consume her, and the public's skepticism only sharpened the ache. But what cut deepest was the indifference—the way some dismissed her efforts, shrugged off the risks, acted as if her sacrifices meant nothing. She saw it in the impatience of those who refused masks, in the casual dismissal of lives lost, in the thankless grind of shifts that stretched too long. It stung, but it didn't break her. Instead of stepping away, she pressed on, carrying

not just her own burden but the weight left behind by colleagues lost to the pandemic. Her work became a quiet rebellion—proof that even in the face of disregard, she would not yield.

Day after day, these dedicated individuals pour their hearts into their work, often sacrificing personal comfort to serve others. Despite facing resistance and skepticism from the public, healthcare workers do not stop educating and treating patients. This consistent patient education can be a lifeline for improving mental health nationally and globally.

Therapy – A Sign of Weakness?

People clung to whatever they could to get through the days. Some buried themselves in work, others took up baking, online shopping, or binge-watching shows just to fill the silence. But for many, coping meant reaching for something stronger—something that dulled the fear, the boredom, the crushing loneliness. Rashadah Jordan, a physician associate in psychiatry, saw it unfold in real-time. Her patients came to her not just with anxiety or depression, but with the weight of habits they couldn't shake.

Therapy was an option, but for many, even saying they needed help felt like an admission of failure. They had been taught that struggling meant weakness, that they should push through on their own. So instead, they held onto what was breaking them. And as the weeks dragged on, what started as a way to get by became something they couldn't let go of—until it wasn't just the virus they were fighting, but themselves.

Even as a psychiatrist, Rashadah wasn't immune to the weight of it all. She felt the same isolation, the same creeping uncertainty that her patients described. The long days blurred together, and the fear of what might come next settled deep in her chest. She listened to their struggles, fully understanding how overwhelming it was to navigate a world that no longer felt stable.

To reduce my anxiety levels, I would go for walks and drives, but they became old. Since I was also working from home, I felt trapped. The closed walls confined and locked me.

Rashadah turned to walks and drives, hoping movement would quiet the unease. But as the days blurred together, the same streets, the same scenery, the same routine lost their effect. The walls of her home, once a place of comfort, began to feel like they were closing in. Working remotely only reinforced the isolation, each day a cycle of confinement with no real escape.

That feeling wasn't hers alone—it was a reality for so many of us. As the pandemic unfolded, our worlds shrank. Our plans unraveled. The future we had worked toward suddenly felt out of reach. New graduates were stripped of the ceremonies they had earned. Families struggled without an income. Children longed for friendships beyond a screen. Travel plans disappeared. Weddings were postponed. Entrance exams delayed. Babysitters and daycare services vanished, forcing parents to juggle impossible responsibilities. Family-owned businesses shuttered, their dreams slipping away with every lost customer. One by one, the markers of stability we had counted on were erased, leaving us all searching for what came next.

A study published in Psychological Science in the Public Interest found that reducing mental health stigma can encourage more people to seek care.[24] Rashadah saw this firsthand—her patients weren't just struggling with anxiety

[24] Corrigan PW, Druss BG, Perlick DA. The Impact of Mental Illness Stigma on Seeking and Participating in Mental Health Care. Psychol Sci Public Interest. 2014 Oct;15(2):37–70.

and depression; they were also battling the fear of being judged for needing help. The study's findings reinforce what she witnessed during the pandemic: stigma remains one of the biggest barriers to mental health care. But the pandemic made things even harder. People were already overwhelmed by the weight of isolation, financial strain, and the uncertainty of what lay ahead. Admitting they needed help felt like just one more burden in a world that was already too much to handle.

Rashadah watched as her patients searched for something—anything—to take the edge off. Anxiety, fear, loneliness, boredom. The days dragged, empty and uncertain, and substance use became an easy escape. A drink to soften the fear. A pill to push back the isolation. A quick high to make the hours pass.

Therapy could have helped, but for many, that door had never been open. Admitting they needed help felt like failure, like weakness. That's what they had been taught. So, they turned to what felt easier, what didn't carry shame, what didn't come with judgment. The same stigma that kept them from a therapist's office pushed them toward a bottle, a pipe, or a pill.

She heard it in their voices—the frustration, the exhaustion, the slow unraveling. They wanted to feel better but didn't know how. The pandemic didn't just isolate them; it cornered them. Stripped of connection, of routine, of access to healthier coping mechanisms, they reached for whatever was within arm's length. Even if it hurt them more in the end.

The reluctance to seek therapy because of mental health stigma isn't just a personal struggle. It's a societal issue that we must actively work to dismantle. The truth is that therapy is not a sign of weakness—it's a sign of strength. It takes courage to confront emotions, process trauma, and seek guidance in difficult times. Yet, stigma, fear, and misinformation still prevent millions from getting the help they need. Breaking the stigma starts with us. If you've ever hesitated to seek therapy, remind yourself that taking care of your mental well-being is no different from seeing a doctor for a physical illness. Healthcare professionals, too, must continue advocating for accessible mental health resources, especially for those in vulnerable situations.

An Old Habit

In the pandemic, excess alcohol use became increasingly prevalent, particularly in young adults. People were drinking more, especially when they were alone at home. Their friends and family were not checking in as much, and they did not see that their loved ones were developing jaundice, which is a yellowing of the skin and eyes due to excess alcohol use. Liver disease became more common, and patients delayed seeking care. People treated their anxiety and depression with alcohol, leading to the development of an alcohol use disorder and liver disease, and we are seeing the downstream effects now, and we will continue to see them for years to come.

During the pandemic, Dr. Rita German, a transplant hepatologist at the University of Wisconsin-Madison, noticed a worrying trend. In addition to missed screenings, she observed an increase in patients with liver disease and cancer. Some cases were undiagnosed issues that became progressively worse. Others were due to excess alcohol use caused by multiple factors, including untreated mental health disorders and isolation.

Levels of anxiety and depression were higher than ever. It did not help that the pandemic locked many people in their homes, away from loved ones. Those battling depressive inner thoughts and anxieties now did so in isolation. Or with a few family members or roommates in houses that felt more like prisons than homes. The pandemic was difficult for everyone. Many tried various coping mechanisms. Some pursued a new hobby or passion, such as painting or singing.

Others turned to an old and familiar destructive habit from which they fought to break free.

As isolation deepened and untreated mental health struggles, like depression and anxiety, festered, many turned to alcohol as a way to numb the ache. What started as occasional drinking became more frequent, earlier in the day, and in larger quantities than they ever planned. The need to escape grew stronger with every passing day, and so did the grip of alcohol. But the relief was short-lived. While it temporarily quieted the mental noise, it also dulled the motivation needed to get through everyday tasks, dragging them further into the weight of untreated depression. The cycle deepened. Alcohol, once a way to cope, only worsened the loneliness and anxiety it was meant to ease. The effects spiraled: liver disease took root, and the pressures at work, at home, and in school mounted, each burden heavier than the last.

Along with alcohol use disorder, Dr. German's patients had other health concerns that the pandemic exacerbated. She recalls describing one patient who received a positive result on a colon cancer screening test that searches for large polyps and blood in the stool. After getting the positive test results, the patient received instructions to get a colonoscopy, a procedure to check for polyps and cancer in the colon. While attempting to schedule this exam, Dr. German and her team had difficulty contacting the patient.

By the time the patient finally received her colonoscopy, it was too late. What started as a routine screening had uncovered something far worse: colon cancer, already metastasized to her liver. This wasn't an isolated incident—

it became all too common during the pandemic. As healthcare systems buckled under the pressure of COVID-19, screenings were postponed, routine tests missed, and appointments rescheduled. The result? Patients faced devastating diagnoses—conditions that could have been detected and treated earlier, now more advanced and harder to treat. For many, this delay didn't just change their diagnosis—it stole their chances at early intervention, leaving them to face a future they never should have had to.

Dr. German's experiences during the pandemic have highlighted the far-reaching health impacts beyond the virus, self-quarantine, masks, isolation, and vaccines. These stories serve as a powerful tool to increase awareness about growing issues of alcohol use disorder and the importance of timely cancer screenings. By sharing these experiences, we empower you to take charge of your health and schedule your next check-up as part of preventative care.

An article published in the International Journal of Environmental Research and Public Health showed that, during the pandemic, people began purchasing more drugs than usual, worrying they may not have access to make purchases later.[25] People also started using substances alone without others around them. This isolation significantly increased the risk of a life-threatening overdose because no one could intervene to save them if needed.

---

[25] Jeffers A, Meehan AA, Barker J, Asher A, Montgomery MP, Bautista G, et al. Impact of Social Isolation during the COVID-19 Pandemic on Mental Health, Substance Use, and Homelessness: Qualitative Interviews with Behavioral Health Providers. IJERPH. 2022 Sep 25;19(19):12120.

For some, addiction made an already precarious situation worse. Evictions, job losses, and social isolation pushed people further to the margins. A missed rent payment turned into an eviction notice. A shelter bed turned into a spot on the sidewalk. For many, there was no safety net—only rules that seemed impossible to follow.

A man stood in the lobby of the clinic, gripping the edge of the counter like it was the only thing keeping him upright. His mask was damp, his voice raw. "I'm too old for this," he said, choking on the words. "I can't stay on the street. I'm too old. And none of the shelters will take me back because I haven't had the COVID-19 test."

The rules had changed overnight. Shelters, once a last refuge, now had new conditions—no test, no bed. Some had figured it out, found a way to get tested, waited in lines that wrapped around city blocks. Others, like him, didn't know where to go. No phone to check for testing sites, no bus fare to get there even if he did. The system had no answers for people like him.

So, they wandered. Some found doorways to sleep in, alleys with just enough cover to keep the wind from cutting through their coats. Some pleaded at shelter doors, hoping someone would bend the rules, let them in, just this once. But the rules were the rules, and the doors stayed shut.

He wasn't asking for much. Just a bed. A warm place to sleep. A few hours where he didn't have to worry about where to go next. But the pandemic had taken even that. He wiped his face with a shaking hand, staring down at the floor. "I don't know what to do," he whispered.

And no one had an answer.

The pandemic amplified problems to a degree not expected. By learning this now, we can better serve people experiencing homelessness and those dealing with substance use problems if such a situation ever arises.

Gripped by Substance Abuse

Dr. Monzurul Roni, a neuropharmacologist with a Ph.D. in Pharmaceutical Sciences, shared insights on what drove many people to use substances during the pandemic. Factors like anxiety over finances, loss of support from family, more free time with less to do, and a lack of the warmth that comes from human connection gripped many patients. Faced with mounting stress and nowhere to turn, many saw only two options: seek professional help or numb the pain however they could. But therapy wasn't always an easy choice. Long waitlists, high costs, and the weight of stigma made it feel out of reach. Even before COVID-19, addiction treatment was difficult to access. Public rehab programs were underfunded, private ones were unaffordable, and insurance rarely covered enough sessions to make a real difference. The pandemic only widened the cracks; clinics shut down, counselors were overloaded, and telehealth wasn't an option for those without reliable internet.

The people who needed help the most—low-income workers, those recently released from prison, parents without childcare—were often the ones turned away.

So, for many, substances became the next best thing—a quick escape, a way to quiet the storm, even if just for a little while. Unfortunately, the limited access to mental health services and fear of mental health stigma pushed many toward substance use. Research shows that the number of positive drug tests for fentanyl, cocaine, heroin, and methamphetamine increased [during the pandemic] from previous years.[26]

Our brain has a reward pathway in which drugs produce a pleasurable sensation. When someone consumes a substance like morphine or marijuana, the substance travels to the brain. The brain then releases the neurotransmitter dopamine, the happy hormone. When people find pleasure in these addictive substances, they can get hooked and want more of them.

Dr. Roni explained that addiction often goes hand in hand with an unhealthy lifestyle. Many struggling with substance use fall into erratic eating habits, get little sleep, and rarely exercise—patterns that gradually wear down the body, weakening the immune system and making it even harder to break the cycle. Their persistent substance abuse leads to vitamin and mineral deficiencies, possibly making them more susceptible to COVID-19.

Quitting wasn't as simple as just making the decision to stop. The body fights back. The nausea hits first, rolling through in waves. Then came the feeling of ants crawling under the skin. Sleep was impossible. The body begged for relief, for just one more hit to make it all stop.

The awareness of harm is there, but withdrawal overrides logic. When the body is in distress, when every muscle aches, when sleep is impossible, and nausea comes in waves,

---

[26] Wainwright JJ, Mikre M, Whitley P, Dawson E, Huskey A, Lukowiak A, et al. Analysis of Drug Test Results Before and After the US Declaration of a National Emergency Concerning the COVID-19 Outbreak. JAMA. 2020 Oct 27;324(16):1674.

the mind fixates on one thing: relief. In those moments, the need to escape the suffering outweighs everything else, pulling people back into the cycle of use despite their best intentions.

Alongside substance abuse, people living alone found it challenging to seek help during the pandemic, as many social and mental health services were unavailable. With healthcare providers focused on COVID-19 cases, access to care for substance abuse issues became limited. For many struggling with addiction, the pandemic brought more than just isolation—it took away jobs, support systems, and loved ones. Grief and uncertainty replaced stability, making recovery feel even further out of reach.

Addiction does not discriminate, but society does. While substance use disorder affects people across all backgrounds, the way it is treated—or punished—depends heavily on race, class, and social status. The opioid crisis, largely affecting white and suburban communities, has been met with a public health response: treatment programs, funding for mental health services, and discussions about harm reduction. But when crack cocaine devastated Black and Latino communities in the 1980s and 1990s, the response wasn't compassion—it was mass incarceration.[27]

The pandemic magnified these disparities. Black and Latino individuals were more likely to lack health insurance, and more likely to live in communities with underfunded

---

[27] Drake J, Charles C, Kwende M. Exploring the impact of the opioid epidemic in Black and Hispanic communities in the United States. *Ther Adv Drug Saf.* 2020 Aug 31;11:2050324520940428. doi: 10.1177/2050324520940428.

healthcare systems.[28] When substance use became a coping mechanism for pandemic-induced stress, access to treatment was anything but equal. Wealthier individuals had the option of private rehab, while low-income communities, particularly communities of color, were left with long waitlists, overburdened public clinics, and few resources to support recovery.

Even law enforcement responses reflected this divide. White individuals caught with opioids were often diverted to treatment programs, while Black and Latino individuals faced higher arrest rates and harsher sentencing for drug-related offenses.[29] The war on drugs never ended.

To regain motivation and break free from addiction, Dr. Roni stressed the importance of reconnecting with loved ones. He urged those struggling to use virtual technology to bridge the physical distance, to seek out conversations not just for distraction but for healing—discussions about peace, harmony, and love that could reawaken their sense of self. These connections weren't just about passing the time; they were a way to stimulate cognitive function, ease emotional burdens, and restore a sense of belonging. Addiction doesn't vanish overnight, and recovery is never a straight path, but Dr. Roni understood that even the smallest moments of connection could plant the seeds of hope, giving individuals

---

[28] National Research Council (US) Panel on Race, Ethnicity, and Health in Later Life; Bulatao RA, Anderson NB, editors. *Understanding Racial and Ethnic Differences in Health in Late Life: A Research Agenda* [Internet]. Washington (DC): National Academies Press (US); 2004. Chapter 10, Health Care. Available from: https://www.ncbi.nlm.nih.gov/books/NBK24693/

[29] Volkow ND. Addiction should be treated, not penalized. *Neuropsychopharmacology*. 2021 Nov;46(12):2048-2050. doi: 10.1038/s41386-021-01087-2. Epub 2021 Aug 17. PMID: 34404909; PMCID: PMC8369862.

the strength to speak their pain and take the first tentative steps toward healing.

The pandemic has taught us that human connections are a cornerstone of overcoming substance addiction and reducing the risk of relapse. Looking ahead, healthcare providers can take proactive steps to educate patients about nurturing human connections, whether through support groups, community programs, or reconnecting with loved ones. Breaking addiction isn't just about willpower. It's about building systems that make recovery possible. That means funding community outreach programs, expanding harm reduction services, and treating substance use disorder like the public health crisis it is—not a personal failing.

Some states have started to make changes. In Rhode Island, the first state-run safe consumption site opened, providing a space for people to use substances under medical supervision, reducing overdose deaths.[30] In California, grant programs now fund peer-support networks, connecting recovering addicts with mentors who have walked the same road. These efforts aren't perfect, but they recognize one critical truth: no one recovers alone.

If the pandemic taught us anything, it's that isolation can break people. But connection—real, intentional connection—can help put them back together.

Physicians can amplify these efforts by integrating relationship-building strategies into treatment plans. The call

---

[30] Rhode Island Department of Health. Harm Reduction Center Pilot Program. Providence (RI): Rhode Island Department of Health;. Available from: https://health.ri.gov/sites/g/files/xkgbur1006/files/publications/factsheets/Harm-Reduction-Center-Pilot-Program.pdf

to action is clear: we must prioritize connection in the fight against substance abuse.

Too Much Time to Think

Dr. Erin Thase, who holds a Ph.D. in school psychology, had built her career around face-to-face connections. As an outpatient psychologist at UC Health in Cincinnati, Ohio, she worked with patients in rooms designed for conversation—quiet, steady spaces where healing happened in the pauses as much as in the words. In the fall of 2019, she moved into an administrative role, trading direct patient care for the responsibility of overseeing an entire psychotherapy department.

Six months later, everything changed as the pandemic unfolded. Then came the order: move the entire psychotherapy department online. And do it in two weeks.

Therapists who had built their practice on presence—on the subtle shifts in posture, the unspoken cues, the moments when a patient finally exhaled—were now staring at screens. Sessions were marked by technical glitches, frozen faces, and conversations cut short by bad connections. Some patients adapted, learning to open up through a pixelated world. Others disappeared, unable or unwilling to turn therapy into another virtual meeting.

Dr. Thase wasn't just managing a transition—she was watching a field built on human connection fracture under the weight of isolation. The question wasn't just whether therapy could be done online. It was whether it could still work.

She treated between 30-40 patients every week and observed that many of her patients, whether previously diagnosed or not, were battling mental health issues. The cherry on top was the isolation, which aggravated their symptoms. With a shortage of mental health clinicians and a rise in mental health cases, many existing clinicians, including Dr. Thase, found themselves overwhelmed throughout the process.

People were in a state of panic, and they wanted immediate answers. As a mental health clinician, sometimes it would get very tiring to talk about COVID-19 all the time.

As Dr. Thase saw an increasing number of patients during the pandemic, she acknowledged that she could access intimate areas of her patients' lives. Patients trusted her enough to express their emotional and mental traumas to her, which they did not feel comfortable sharing with anyone else. Over this time, she realized the importance of setting firm boundaries inside and outside her workspace. She realized that it is not appropriate to carry her patients' traumas and struggles with her after she leaves the clinic or moves on to the next task of the day.

I cannot be the center of their life, and they cannot be the center of my life. If I try to fix all my clients 24/7, there will be 160 more who will show up at my door tomorrow. I can only be in control of what I can control; all I can control is what I recommend in the space I share with the patient. Ultimately, they must take all that information and decide how they want their lives to go.

Trying to create boundaries, Dr. Thase also sometimes struggled to relate to her patient's traumas because she had not always experienced the same stress as her client despite being a psychologist. Sometimes, when Dr. Thase met with a patient going through something devastating—like a divorce—she would dive into research, mapping out mental patterns to better understand their pain. She wanted to meet them where they were, to grasp not just the facts of their situation but the emotions behind it.

But in her interactions, she observed that many patients weren't looking for solutions. They weren't asking for strategies or advice—they just needed to be heard. Their lives had unraveled too quickly for them to process. Daily routines had crumbled, relationships strained. Some worried about losing their jobs, others about losing their marriages. The pandemic didn't just threaten their health—it threatened everything stable, everything familiar. And in those sessions, sometimes the best thing Dr. Thase could do was listen and be present with them, offering the space they needed to feel seen, to feel understood, even when no immediate answers existed.

Even though it triggered anxiety, this period also served as a reminder for people to evaluate aspects of their relationships that they would not have done otherwise. Dr. Thase emphasized that many patients had communication problems. Some dealt with miscommunication, and others experienced a complete lack of communication and trust in their relationships. Unfortunately, they previously ignored those issues because they were distracted by their professional hassle and the drive of social life. Compared to concerns about their career and social life, many of their relationship issues seemed insignificant to them until the pandemic struck, so they had no choice but to face their relationship issues.

When they were left alone with their thoughts, they began to ask necessary questions like, am I content with my relationship, or do I want to spend my whole life with this person? Those were tough questions that we avoided all our lives.

During the journey to ease her patients' struggles, the coping mechanisms Dr. Thase observed in her patients—technology, isolation, distraction, and excessive sleep—were not exclusive to them. These habits mirrored the ways many healthcare providers tried to manage their own stress. Therapists, psychologists, and physicians weren't immune to the emotional weight of the pandemic. They, too, faced uncertainty, burnout, and the psychological toll of supporting patients through crisis after crisis.

Since they relied on the same pre-pandemic coping mechanisms, they thought the same strategies would also work during the pandemic. When COVID-19 struck, and they were alone in their homes, they streamed content for hours and overslept often.

Technology, isolation, distraction, and sleep can be effective but can easily become maladaptive. Relying on these as your only way to cope with overwhelming uncertainty and emotional dysregulation was not enough for most people, and started to create issues in all areas of their lives.

To ease her colleagues' anxiety, she and her team created groups of two to three people who met weekly to discuss burnout. They also incorporated virtual meditations and happy hours in their routines. Many of her colleagues participated in virtual conferences hosted by the American Medical Association (AMA), a professional organization for physicians and medical students dedicated to advancing the science of medicine. These conferences provided a platform for peers to support each other with both professional and personal challenges they faced. The weekly check-ins reminded providers they were not fighting this battle alone.

Although the pandemic overburdened clinicians with responsibilities, it paved the way for more psychotherapy-related practices, allowing more patients to benefit. Before COVID-19, some insurance companies did not cover telehealth psychotherapy and psychiatric services, and some licensing boards refused to endorse any mental health services on virtual platforms. Due to HIPAA regulations, the government stated that no platforms were secure enough to protect patient conversations in a virtual space. When the COVID-19 pandemic struck, these regulations were lifted, allowing clinicians to practice psychotherapy virtually. Insurance began covering more costs for various therapies, and therapists were able to treat patients outside of their practicing state more easily.

Psychologists had always been bound by state lines. A therapist licensed in Ohio could treat patients in Columbus or Cleveland but not across the river in Kentucky, even if they were just a few miles apart. The rules were rigid, and for people living in rural areas, that meant access to care was often limited, sometimes nonexistent.

Then came PsyPact, an agreement that allowed psychologists to practice across multiple states. Suddenly, a therapist in Ohio could see patients in other participating states, breaking down the invisible borders that had long restricted access to care. For those living in small towns and isolated communities, it was a lifeline. Before, therapy often meant driving hours to the nearest provider—if one even existed nearby. Now, all they needed was a screen. Considering this, Dr. Thase made her services more accessible and available to her patients via different platforms. She expanded her practice and provided therapy to her patients from the comfort of their homes.

Working in psychology, Dr. Thase empathized with her patients' concerns. She admitted with utmost honesty and sincerity that her knowledge in her field was not enough for her to relate to every traumatic experience her patients underwent. Even though she could not entirely alleviate their discomfort, she still did her best when she was there with them.

A 2020 study published in Healthcare (Basel) showed how telehealth, particularly in the mental health sector, became a lifeline for both patients and clinicians during this COVID-19 pandemic.[31] This period forced healthcare systems, like the one Dr. Thase worked within, to quickly adopt virtual platforms to continue providing care while ensuring the safety of both patients and healthcare providers. According to the study, telehealth platforms have been

[31] Bouabida K, Lebouché B, Pomey MP. Telehealth and COVID-19 Pandemic: An Overview of the Telehealth Use, Advantages, Challenges, and Opportunities during COVID-19 Pandemic. Healthcare (Basel). 2022 Nov 16;10(11):2293.

pivotal in maintaining continuity of care by using multipurpose technology to connect patients and health professionals remotely. The immediate transition to telehealth services was necessary to combat the challenges posed by physical distancing measures, which not only limited in-person consultations but also contributed to an increased demand for mental health support due to heightened anxiety, isolation, and stress among the general population.

Dr. Thase observed that many of her patients were struggling with mental health issues that were exacerbated by the pandemic. These issues ranged from anxiety and depression to more complex trauma responses, often tied to the emotional weight of the pandemic. As the study points out, telehealth platforms became crucial in offering psychological services remotely, reducing the spread of COVID-19 while still providing patients with the therapy they needed. The study highlighted challenges associated with telehealth during lockdowns, including concerns over confidentiality, data security, and the loss of in-person interaction that many patients find essential in therapeutic settings. Dr. Thase, too, faced the challenge of adapting her practice to this new virtual medium, all while ensuring that her patients continued to feel heard, supported, and understood.

Mental health care had never been built to handle a crisis of this scale. It was a system patched together with long waitlists, insurance loopholes, and overworked providers. When in-person therapy shut down, telehealth became the only option. For some, it was a lifeline. For others, it was a reminder of what was missing—a therapist's steady presence, the quiet comfort of a room that wasn't their own.

Dr. Thase and her colleagues knew the system wasn't just stretched—it was breaking. If providers weren't okay, how could they care for their patients? So, they leaned on each other, forming small support groups, sharing the weight of burnout in the only way they could—together.

The pandemic made it clear: mental health care couldn't go back to the way it was. Expanding telehealth was necessary, but it wasn't enough. It had to be sustainable, accessible, built to reach the people who had always been left out. And for those struggling, the lesson was the same as it had always been—enduring isn't the same as healing. Getting through each day wasn't enough. Real survival meant finding connection, seeking help, and understanding that no one was meant to do it alone.

Summary and Reflection

The COVID-19 pandemic peeled back the façade of resilience within healthcare, exposing deep emotional wounds among those on the frontline and laying bare the systemic vulnerabilities that heightened their suffering. The psychological damage healthcare workers endured was neither accidental nor unforeseen—it was the direct result of institutions and policies ill-equipped to manage the relentless demands and moral complexities thrust upon their staff. These narratives force us to confront pressing ethical questions: What duty do we have to protect those who devote their lives to protecting us? How can we restructure our healthcare system to genuinely prioritize the mental health of its workers?

The swift pivot to telemedicine, while initially driven by necessity, uncovered significant potential for improving mental health care access, particularly in underserved communities. However, it also exposed the need to refine remote mental health interventions to effectively detect and manage nuanced psychological conditions. As we embrace telehealth moving forward, policymakers must ensure equitable digital access to mental health services and resources, preventing digital divides from compounding existing disparities.

The pandemic revealed truths about burnout and the urgency for robust mental health support within healthcare institutions. Preventive measures, like regular emotional check-ins, peer support groups, and psychological first aid training, must become standard practice. Dr. Atkinson's morning huddles offer an example, but broader systemic change is essential. Policies must mandate institutional responsibility for healthcare worker mental health, shifting the burden from individual resilience to organizational accountability.

Ethical dilemmas faced by healthcare workers during the pandemic further magnified mental distress. Constantly navigating decisions around scarce resources, patient care priorities, and personal safety eroded their mental well-being. Clear ethical frameworks and strong psychological support systems must be embedded within healthcare policies to help professionals navigate moral distress without lasting psychological damage.

Technological innovations, such as virtual ICUs, transformed healthcare delivery, yet simultaneously risked depersonalizing patient-provider interactions, potentially exacerbating isolation and emotional disconnection. Integrating empathetic, human-centered design into telehealth platforms is crucial to balance efficiency with compassion, ensuring technology remains a bridge rather than a barrier to mental health.

For students, pre-professionals, and emerging leaders, these lessons point toward actionable commitments: normalizing conversations about mental health, actively advocating for institutional policy changes, and championing the implementation of robust psychological support structures. Students and emerging leaders should foster environments that openly address mental health stigma, promote therapy as an essential practice, and actively engage in community-building to create sustainable support networks.

Ultimately, the pandemic's mental health crisis urges us to rethink healthcare not just as physical treatment, but as holistic support systems embedded in policy, ethics, and empathy. Recognizing the emotional sacrifices of healthcare workers compels us to prioritize mental health support, enabling survival, genuine healing and resilience in the face of future challenges.

Discussion Questions

1. How can the integration of mental health care into everyday health practices be strengthened to ensure that crises like COVID-19 don't exacerbate underlying issues, and what systemic changes are needed to support this integration?

2. What targeted strategies, including education and policy reforms, could help reshape public perceptions of mental health care so that seeking therapy is recognized as a strength rather than a weakness?

3. In light of the rapid shift to telehealth during the pandemic, what measures can be taken to enhance virtual mental health services so that they foster genuine human connection and trust rather than merely serving as a temporary fix?

4. Considering the emotional toll and burnout experienced by healthcare providers, what policies or support systems should be implemented to protect their mental well-being and ensure a sustainable, compassionate workforce in future crises?

5. With isolation, substance abuse, and increased stress contributing to a widespread mental health crisis, how can communities build resilient support networks that address both immediate needs and long-term emotional recovery?

Part 3: Health Disparities and Inequities

Who Was Left Behind?

Introduction

Long before the COVID-19 pandemic, systemic healthcare disparities had been inflicting deep wounds in marginalized communities. Racial and ethnic minorities, immigrants, low-income families, indigenous populations, individuals with disabilities, and more have experienced a healthcare system riddled with inequities. These groups often faced reduced access to quality care, economic barriers, and a lack of culturally competent services that acknowledged their unique needs. Social determinants of health—such as inadequate housing, environmental hazards, and limited educational and employment opportunities—have historically set the stage for poorer health outcomes and contributed to a cycle of disadvantage.

Historically, these inequities were not just statistical anomalies but lived realities. During the HIV/AIDS epidemic in the 1980s, for example, individuals with diverse sexual preferences were impacted by underfunded public health responses. The crisis not only devastated countless lives but showcased the undermined access to quality care. Marginalized groups, faced both the direct threat of the virus and systemic discrimination within healthcare systems that often overlooked their specific needs.

For people of color, the history of mistreatment in healthcare is long and painful. The infamous Tuskegee Syphilis Study,[32] in which Black men were deceived and denied treatment, is one of the most notorious examples. Such abuses were not isolated incidents; they form part of a

[32] Vonderlehr RA, Clark T, Wenger OC, Heller JR. Untreated syphilis in the male Negro. J Venereal Dis Inf. 1936;17:260-265.

broader pattern of exploitation and neglect. For instance, the story of Henrietta Lacks, whose cells were taken without her consent and used for groundbreaking medical research, highlights the profound lack of respect and ethical treatment afforded to many African Americans.[33] Additionally, indigenous communities have faced forced sterilizations and discriminatory policies that stripped them of their autonomy over their own bodies, further entrenching a legacy of distrust and marginalization.[34]

These historical injustices have sown deep seeds of mistrust towards the medical establishment. Research shows that decades of systemic neglect and underrepresentation in the healthcare workforce have significantly fueled skepticism among racial minorities, contributing to vaccine hesitancy and reluctance to seek medical help even when needed. Such experiences reveal how harmful societal attitudes and institutional practices can lead to long-term adverse health outcomes, as well as the persistent barriers that prevent marginalized communities from receiving equitable care.

At the same time, other groups experienced parallel struggles. Indigenous populations and communities of color have long borne the brunt of environmental injustices, living in areas with higher pollution levels and fewer resources, which have exacerbated chronic health conditions.[35] The intersection of economic hardship, environmental factors,

---

[33] Skloot R. The Immortal Life of Henrietta Lacks. New York: Crown Publishing; 2010.

[34] National Library of Medicine. Native Voices timeline. Bethesda (MD): U.S. National Library of Medicine. Available from: https://www.nlm.nih.gov/nativevoices/timeline/543.html.

[35] Berberian AG, Gonzalez DJX, Cushing LJ. Racial disparities in climate change-related health effects in the United States. Curr Environ Health Rep. 2022 Sep;9(3):451-464. doi: 10.1007/s40572-022-00360-w.

and systemic discrimination has created a multi-layered challenge that continues to affect these communities profoundly.

The arrival of COVID-19 did not create these disparities; it merely brought them into sharper focus. The pandemic amplified longstanding issues, highlighting how economic instability, inadequate healthcare access, and pervasive discrimination left many communities disproportionately vulnerable. While COVID-19 exposed these systemic shortcomings to a broader audience, it also provided an opportunity to reexamine and challenge the deeply entrenched inequities that have long affected marginalized groups.

In essence, the narrative of healthcare disparities is one that spans generations, marked by the unequal distribution of resources. Addressing these issues requires acknowledging the environmental and social determinants that have long affected indigenous and low-income communities. By understanding these intertwined histories, we can better appreciate the urgent need for comprehensive reforms that not only address current disparities but also dismantle the systemic barriers that persist today.

As you continue exploring these chapters, consider this guiding question: "How can our understanding of historical and ongoing healthcare inequities inform practical steps to create a more just and inclusive healthcare system for all communities?"

Reflect on the enduring impact of past injustices and think about how collective action, informed policy, and individual advocacy can work together to transform a system that has long marginalized vulnerable groups. Let this question inspire you to delve deeper, challenge established norms and envision solutions that prioritize equity and compassion at every level of healthcare.

More Than a White Coat

Dr. Roma Amin, a family medicine physician, worked relentlessly to meet the needs of her patients during the pandemic. Many of them were people of color from under-resourced communities.

Before the pandemic, some of her patients juggled multiple jobs, piecing together long shifts to keep their families afloat. But when COVID-19 hit, the struggle changed. Childcare disappeared. Aging parents needed care, but visits carried the risk of exposure. Most couldn't afford to work from home—essential workers with no choice but to show up, even when showing up meant putting their health on the line. Dr. Amin saw these pressures unfold in real-time, knowing that for some, the pandemic wasn't just a crisis—it was the breaking point.

She had seen hardship before, even fought against policies that made life harder for her patients. Long before the virus spread, she had testified against House Bill 178, pushing back against legislation that expanded gun access without safety measures.[36] She wasn't speaking in hypotheticals. These were her patients—the young woman shot by her husband, now facing a lifetime of pain; the pregnant mother who lost her partner to a stray bullet, left to raise a child who would never meet his father; the woman who went grocery shopping with her family and walked

[36] Amin R. Testimony in opposition to House Bill 178 [Internet]. Ohio Legislative Information Systems; 2019 Jun 5. Available from: https://search-prod.lis.state.oh.us/api/v2/general_assembly_133/committees/cmte_h_federalism_1/meetings/cmte_h_federalism_1_2019-06-05-0930_656/testimony/3980/uploaded-doc/

away a widow, too deep in grief to care for her son. She had treated them, listened to their stories, and witnessed firsthand how violence and failed policies tore their lives apart. There were wounds no doctor could heal, losses no treatment could undo.

Then came the pandemic, taking everything that was already fragile and making it worse. The same families she had fought for, were suddenly in free fall. The virus didn't just threaten their health—it took their jobs, their stability, their ability to access care. Pay rent or pay for medicine. Keep food on the table or keep the lights on.

Dr. Amin didn't stop fighting. She wrote, she spoke, she pushed back against policies that ignored the most vulnerable. Because she knew that when the system failed, it wasn't lawmakers or lobbyists who paid the price. It was her patients—the families sitting across from her, searching for answers she didn't always have. The people who, long before the pandemic, had already been left behind.

I had a patient whom I saw for many years for chronic disease management. Several years of polysubstance use had led to her severe COPD and heart failure. She was the primary caregiver for her grandson because his mother—her daughter—had an alcohol use disorder and was unable to care for him safely. Both the daughter and grandson had also established care with me before the pandemic, and we were working together to connect the daughter with resources for her alcohol use. During the pandemic, the daughter's alcohol consumption increased, making it harder for all of them to access the care they needed. Ultimately, the stress became too much for the grandmother to handle, and she passed away during the pandemic due to complications from heart disease. The grandson and mother lost their rock, leaving the grandson without a stable caregiver.

This loving grandmother was torn between her responsibilities to care for her grandson, seek help for her daughter, and prioritize her health needs. She had no choice but to work multiple jobs to provide for her family's basic needs, and the toll of it all became too much. While overworking herself, she eventually passed away from heart disease. Unfortunately, this kind of tragedy is all too common and has a rippling impact on families and friends.

Dr. Amin provided a space for her patients to express their needs. She partnered with them to access resources to achieve their goals. Whether listening to a patient mourn the loss of a loved one, empathizing with patients about their struggles of paying for medication, or advocating for more equitable healthcare access, Dr. Amin saw this as her role in improving the health of her community.

Looking back on this chapter, it's clear how deeply stress shaped people's lives—physically and emotionally. When we experience stress, our bodies release cortisol, a hormone designed to help us respond to danger. In short bursts, cortisol is useful, sharpening focus and fueling the body's fight-or-flight response. But when stress becomes chronic, as it did for so many during the pandemic, cortisol levels stay elevated for too long. This constant flood of stress hormones throws the body off balance, suppressing the immune system and making people more vulnerable to illness.

The pandemic only made this worse. People lived in a near-constant state of stress, worrying about job security, family health, and an uncertain future. As cortisol levels stayed high, the body's ability to fight infection weakened—at the worst possible time. Some coped by eating more, exercising less, which increased weight, a physical response to prolonged stress. Others, consumed by anxiety, lost their appetites and lost weight, their struggles often going unnoticed. Whether through excess or depletion, the body bore the weight of survival, showing in ways that few stopped to recognize.

The pandemic affected lives in countless ways. Weight gain, weight loss, addiction, alcohol abuse, and eating disorders surged, especially among young people already navigating the pressures of systemic inequality. These struggles weren't just personal—they were shaped by limited access to healthcare, financial instability, and environments that offered few resources for mental well-being.

Beyond the physical toll of COVID-19, the pandemic had a hidden effect on mental health, particularly in communities where access to mental health support was already scarce. The rise of apps like TikTok, combined with extended isolation, meant that young people spent more time online, constantly comparing themselves to social media figures who lived vastly different realities. For many, this exposure deepened insecurities and reinforced feelings of inadequacy, especially in communities that already faced societal pressure to prove their worth. We are only beginning to understand the lasting impact of these challenges, but as research continues, we hope to uncover just how deeply the pandemic shaped the mental and physical health of these communities.

A review by Wachtler et al. highlights how infection risk during the pandemic varied across socioeconomic groups, with those in more privileged positions facing lower exposure and better protection compared to under-resourced communities.[37] This disparity echoes the 1995 Chicago Heat Wave, where survival was influenced by social and economic privilege. In both crises, those with fewer resources faced the highest risks because of systemic barriers that left them vulnerable. During the pandemic, those with stable jobs and the ability to work from home could shelter safely, while others—essential workers, those living in crowded housing, and people without homes—had no such option. They were forced into exposure, increasing their chances of contracting the virus simply to survive.

People from socioeconomically disadvantaged groups have a higher infection risk, are more frequently hospitalized and receive intensive care, and also have higher COVID-19 mortality rates than people from socioeconomically more privileged groups.

Healthcare providers don't just treat symptoms—they see the full weight of what their patients are up against. They hear the exhaustion in a mother's voice as she juggles two jobs and still can't afford childcare. They watch as an elderly patient hesitates to refill a prescription, rationing their

[37] Wachtler B, Michalski N, Nowossadeck E, Diercke M, Wahrendorf M, Santos-Hövener C, et al. Socioeconomic inequalities and COVID-19 – A review of the current international literature. 2020 Oct 9 [cited 2025 Jan 28]; Available from: https://edoc.rki.de/handle/176904/6997

medication because the cost is too high. They sit with families who have lost loved ones to preventable tragedies, knowing that better policies could have changed the outcome. They don't just read about disparities in reports—they witness them unfold in real time, in real lives.

Dr. Amin understood this. She knew that medicine alone couldn't fix what was broken. So, she spoke up. She testified against policies that put her patients at risk, pushing back against lawmakers who didn't see what she saw. She fought for the people sitting in her exam room.

Doctors like her are more than caregivers. They are the bridge between suffering and change, the ones who carry their patients' stories into the rooms where decisions are made. Their voices matter—not because they hold titles, but because they bring the weight of real, lived experience. And in a world where those most affected often don't have the platform, social capital, or power to speak for themselves, that kind of advocacy isn't just important—it's essential.

The Lesser of Two Evils

We still offered screening mammograms for everyone but sent out a disclaimer saying that we would understand if patients wanted to delay them. At that point, it was a risk-benefit decision because COVID-19 was so new, and with no vaccine, there was a risk of someone contracting COVID-19 from entering our facilities. So, we had to decide: Is the risk of COVID worth catching breast cancer early, or should we delay the mammograms?

Dr. Tiffany Chan, a breast radiologist with training in diagnostic radiology specializing in breast imaging at UCLA, found herself battling between the lesser of two evils: seeing patients to diagnose breast cancer and risk COVID-19 infection or delaying screenings to prevent COVID-19 exposure and risk breast cancers going undetected, and even worse, metastasizing.

The American Cancer Society (ACS) recommends that average-risk women between ages 40 and 44 have the option to start getting mammograms every year to catch breast cancer in its early stages.[38] For women at high risk, the ACS recommends beginning mammograms at age 30. It's crucial to remember that specialists can develop a treatment plan for cancers when they can feel them but do not advise waiting until cancers produce symptoms. The fear of visiting doctors

[38] American Cancer Society Recommendations for the Early Detection of Breast Cancer. American Cancer Society [Internet]. Available from: https://www.cancer.org/cancer/types/breast-cancer/screening-tests-and-early-detection/american-cancer-society-recommendations-for-the-early-detection-of-breast-cancer.html

during the COVID-19 pandemic led many patients to neglect their screening mammograms, leaving their cancers undiagnosed and leading to unfortunate outcomes.

Seeing fewer patients, Dr. Chan had fewer studies to read and biopsies to perform. Biopsies are medical procedures where physicians obtain body tissue samples to check for the presence of disease. As a result of seeing fewer patients, Dr. Chan and her team ended up temporarily shutting down some of their outpatient centers. However, after the COVID-19 outbreak subsided and the vaccine was introduced, she and many breast radiologists encouraged people through newsletters, emails, word of mouth, and news to get screening mammograms and saw an influx of patients. It was great news that patients were returning for their appointments and getting their needed mammograms. Unfortunately, it became clear that there had been a delay in diagnosis for many patients.

Sadly, the fear of contracting COVID-19 was not the only reason for postponing a screening mammogram. One story involves a patient who did not see her physician for a year because she had spent 2020–2021 looking after her husband, who had contracted COVID-19.

I had a patient in her late 60s or early 70s who was missing appointments due to taking care of her husband, who contracted COVID-19. By the time we saw her, she had a very suspicious mass and needed a biopsy. She explained that she would have visited me earlier but had to look after her husband. So, she was taking care of him and neglecting herself.

This patient's story is nothing out of the ordinary and depicts one of the many insurmountable sacrifices people made during the pandemic. Some healthcare workers sacrificed by renting out hotel rooms, living in vehicles, and being far away from their spouses, children, and grandchildren. Others chose not to work for fear of bringing the deadly virus home to the immunocompromised and little ones. These are sacrifices that they made for the welfare of their families and patients.

An article published in Cancer Cell that shows chronic stress promotes the release of certain hormones that induce a type of white blood cell called neutrophils to form neutrophil extracellular traps (NETs). These NETs can inadvertently help cancer spread throughout the body; a process known as metastasis.[39]

Knowing this now, we can see how stressful times like a pandemic can increase the likelihood of cancer spreading, so we should take precautions and implement a plan to mitigate our stress levels when they rise. To reduce stress, we can engage in physical activity, eat a balanced diet, have a daily routine, pursue hobbies or creative outlets such as painting, gardening, and staying connected socially. These things can help us navigate the mental and emotional challenges of pandemics or other crises and make a difference in overall well-being.

[39] He XY, Gao Y, Ng D, Michalopoulou E, George S, Adrover JM, et al. Chronic stress increases metastasis via neutrophil-mediated changes to the microenvironment. Cancer Cell. 2024 Mar;42(3):474-486.e12.

A Breast Surgeon's Journey as a New Mother

When Dr. Ann Chuang, a fellowship-trained breast cancer surgeon in Montclair, NJ, became a mother during the pandemic, her life revolved around two anxieties: protecting her newborn from COVID-19 and providing care for women facing delayed breast cancer diagnoses. Both were shaped by isolation. Her baby, raised in a world of masks and quarantine, had limited exposure to people beyond her immediate family. Meanwhile, her patients—many from under-resourced communities—were left without access to early cancer screenings, their health concerns sidelined as clinics shut down. Both the youngest and most vulnerable suffered the consequences of a world that had suddenly become unreachable.

It is scary managing life as a physician in the pandemic and becoming a new mother because I don't want to be the person who brings home the disease to my newborn. Usually, we would have a nanny or daycare facility, but with the pandemic and not having enough information, I really depended on my family to help raise my child.

It was scary for my child because she had never seen people outside—never seen non-Asians or blonde hair—and she would get scared. Many babies were home and saw people who only looked like them.

This wasn't an isolated experience. Research shows that early exposure to diverse faces, voices, and environments is crucial for cognitive and emotional development.[40] Babies learn how to process emotions and form social bonds through interactions with different people. When those experiences are limited, children may struggle with anxiety, fear of the unfamiliar, and difficulties adapting to new environments.

Dr. Chuang, like many parents, worried about the long-term effects of this social deprivation. Would these children have trouble building relationships? Would they struggle with social anxiety later in life? The answers are still unfolding, but experts suggest that prolonged isolation during a critical developmental stage may have lasting effects on emotional resilience and social adaptability.

While pandemic-era children missed out on socialization, another group—women facing breast cancer—were also left isolated, but in a far more life-threatening way.

Many women delayed their breast cancer screenings, so we were finding advanced diseases that had progressed to dangerous levels. I once had a breast cancer patient that was transferred to me from another surgeon, and because this patient's care was delayed, her cancer had progressed to stage IV and was beyond curable.

With increasing COVID-19 cases and mortality rates, patients quarantined and were afraid to attend their doctor's appointments. With each surge and new virus variant,

[40] Carnevali L, Gui A, Jones EJH, Farroni T. Face processing in early development: A systematic review of behavioral studies and considerations in times of COVID-19 pandemic. *Front Psychol.* 2022 Feb 18;13:778247. doi: 10.3389/fpsyg.2022.778247. PMID: 35250718; PMCID: PMC8894249.

patients began to miss screenings, surgeries, and opportunities to remove lumps indicative of breast cancer. For patients from wealthier backgrounds, delaying a screening was a matter of rescheduling—but for those in under-resourced communities, it was a question of survival. Many worked essential jobs without paid sick leave, making it nearly impossible to take time off for screenings. Childcare shortages and transportation barriers added another layer of difficulty, leaving many women without a feasible way to seek care.

When patients started to reappear several months later, they often needed more aggressive treatments that had a lower chance of effectively treating the tumor compared to procedures in earlier stages.

Patients usually have four methods to manage their worsening breast cancer, Dr. Chuang explained. These methods are surgery, radiation, chemotherapy, and oral medication. The more advanced the cancer, the more therapy is needed, and this often means that the patient will receive stronger medicines that are not tolerated well. Side effects from medications vary in the level of pain, and some can debilitate the patient to the point that they are almost bedridden. They can cause symptoms like liver failure, low white blood cell count, hair loss, and fatigue.

Facing a suspicious lump meant weighing the risk of delaying care against the danger of exposure to COVID-19. Many, particularly those in under-resourced communities, chose to wait, not because they wanted to, but because they had no safe alternative. By the time they finally sought help, their cancer had progressed, requiring more aggressive treatments with severe side effects—treatments that often left them too weak to work, care for their families, or afford follow-up care. For immunocompromised patients undergoing chemotherapy, the fear of infection was constant. Individuals in racial and ethnic minority groups had lower screening rates than their White counterparts; moreover, the pandemic maintained or exacerbated these existing disparities.[41] What should have been a clear path to treatment became a painful, uncertain battle—one made even harder by financial strain, healthcare barriers, and a system unequipped to protect them.

Like other medical professionals, Dr. Chuang also struggled with a lack of supplies in her office and assessing her patients through televisits. It is difficult to diagnose breast cancer without a tissue specimen, which requires a biopsy gun, a tool not readily available. Numbing medications and implants after surgery were also in short supply. The waiting period to receive biopsy results was increased from three to seven days. Since diagnosing breast cancer requires a physical exam, biopsy, and imaging tests, it was not feasible for Dr. Chuang to assess signs of potential breast cancer through a digital screening during a telehealth visit.

Despite the challenges of the pandemic, Dr. Chuang found ways to balance her roles as a physician and a mother. Adapting to an overburdened healthcare system while caring for a newborn was never easy, but she remained committed

[41] Chung A, Chen Q, Curry W, Felix T, Tuan WJ. Breast Cancer Screening During the COVID-19 Pandemic in the United States: Results From Real-World Health Records Data. Ann Fam Med. 2024 May;22(3):208–14.

to both. She focused on educating her patients, emphasizing the importance of early breast cancer screenings even in the midst of uncertainty. Many of her patients, particularly those from under-resourced communities, had already postponed critical checkups, putting their health at greater risk. She encouraged them to prioritize preventive care, knowing that delayed screenings could mean the difference between a treatable condition and a life-threatening diagnosis.

Understanding that many of her patients were disconnected from in-person healthcare, Dr. Chuang turned to social media to reach them where they were. She used her platform to post videos reminding people to schedule their screenings, recognizing that a simple nudge could prompt someone to take action. But reminders weren't enough—she also took on the role of a myth-buster, tackling misinformation head-on. From false claims about vaccines to misconceptions about breast cancer risks, she used social media to break down complex medical information in a way that was accessible, approachable, and most importantly, trustworthy.

At the same time, she urged her patients to get vaccinated, protect themselves, and slow the spread of COVID-19. She understood that healthcare wasn't just about treatment—it was about prevention, education, and ensuring that people had the resources they needed to stay safe.

But while she worked tirelessly to protect her patients, her own child was growing up in a world shaped by isolation. Like many children of healthcare professionals, Dr. Chuang's baby spent months in a controlled environment, rarely exposed to new people or places. Without the usual interactions that help infants develop social and emotional skills, these pandemic-era children faced challenges that researchers are only beginning to understand.

The long-term effects of this period remain uncertain, but one thing is clear: the impact of the pandemic didn't stop at those who were sick—it reshaped the lives of an entire generation. While pandemic-era children missed out on key social experiences, women who delayed screenings faced even graver consequences.

The pandemic revealed just how interconnected our health truly is. Some had the privilege of working remotely, avoiding exposure, and accessing quality medical care. Others had no such options. In communities where vaccine access was limited and misinformation spread quickly, the responsibility fell on those who could protect themselves to also protect others.

Healthcare is not just an individual choice—it's a collective effort. The more people who receive vaccinations and preventive care, the safer we all become, especially for those most vulnerable. The pandemic showed us the gaps, the inequalities, and the urgent need for change. Now, it's up to all of us to make sure no one is left behind.

HIV vs. COVID-19

During the pandemic, people carried the weight of being untouchable—kept at a distance, avoided, and seen as potential threats. They experienced feelings that echoed the devastating memories of the early HIV/AIDS epidemic. There was a big difference in how these feelings affected marginalized communities of the HIV crisis in the 1980s compared to the COVID-19 pandemic. Back then, in the 1980s, the response was less unified and less proactive, while during COVID-19, the world came together quickly and with a strong sense of community to fight the virus.

At the beginning of the HIV epidemic, the virus was called the "gay plague" or gay-related immunodeficiency disease (GRID).[42] This label led to widespread stigma, isolation, and blame toward those affected. Many people with HIV were marginalized, even by healthcare providers, creating a harsh environment for them.

The fear, uncertainty, and social disruptions experienced during the HIV/AIDS and COVID-19 pandemics highlight a recurring pattern seen across various public health crises throughout history. For instance, during the Spanish Flu pandemic of 1918, widespread panic, social isolation, and misinformation similarly overwhelmed communities globally. These pandemics consistently reveal deeper

[42] Fee E, Krieger N. Understanding AIDS: historical interpretations and the limits of biomedical individualism. Am J Public Health. 1993 Oct;83(10):1477–86.

societal issues, including prejudices, inequitable access to healthcare, and deficiencies in public health infrastructure.

In the 1980s, political and cultural attitudes significantly slowed down responses to HIV/AIDS. Influential policymakers initially ignored the crisis, partly due to stigma against affected groups such as men who have sex with men, intravenous drug users, and sex workers. This neglect resulted in delayed funding for crucial research and treatments, contributing to a higher number of deaths. Activism from groups like ACT UP (AIDS Coalition to Unleash Power) became essential to advocate for recognition, research funding, and compassionate healthcare policies.

In contrast, people with COVID-19 may have faced different levels of societal shame and rejection as those diagnosed with HIV, but that did not mean they were free from stigma. Asian communities, in particular, became targets of racism, violence, and exclusion. As the virus spread, so did misinformation, fueling a surge in anti-Asian rhetoric that blamed individuals, rather than the disease itself, for the pandemic.

This pattern of scapegoating took many forms. Asian people were harassed, assaulted, and treated as permanent outsiders in their own countries. They were denied service at businesses, verbally abused in public spaces, and physically attacked for simply existing. The media and public discourse often pathologized cultural practices, treating Asian customs as dangerous or responsible for the spread of disease. Many faced the ascription of diseased status, where their very identity became synonymous with infection. Others experienced the duality of being both frontline heroes and virus carriers—applauded for their essential work in healthcare and service industries while simultaneously feared and avoided.

The stark difference in public health responses between HIV and COVID-19 also revealed deeper racial and social disparities. Those diagnosed with HIV were met with years of institutional neglect, forced to fight for recognition. Meanwhile, COVID-19 spurred an immediate, large-scale global response—but not all communities benefited equally. While resources poured into vaccine development and treatment, Asian individuals faced the additional burden of defending their humanity against racist attacks.

This wave of xenophobia was not just a momentary backlash; it inflicted lasting psychological and social trauma on Asian communities worldwide. The damage extended beyond individual experiences, reinforcing generational cycles of exclusion and discrimination. If public health responses are to be truly effective, they must not only combat the virus but also dismantle the harmful narratives and racial scapegoating that emerge alongside it.

The HIV and COVID-19 epidemics had significant impacts on the world. However, the epidemics were quite different. Those with HIV fought for long to receive support and funding. In contrast, those with COVID-19 received support and funding much earlier.

Although there have been advances in developing an HIV vaccine, the process is complex due to the nature of the virus. In contrast, scientists created the COVID-19 vaccine at a relatively unprecedented speed.

HIV vaccine development remains uniquely challenging because the virus mutates rapidly, evades the immune system, and integrates itself into human DNA. Decades of research have led to promising trials but no fully effective vaccine yet. Conversely, COVID-19 vaccines benefited from years of prior research on related coronaviruses, like SARS and MERS, and global cooperation facilitated rapid development and emergency approvals within one year. This contrast displays the importance of sustained funding and international collaboration in disease preparedness and vaccine research.

The strategies for preventing transmission of HIV and COVID-19 are also quite different. COVID-19 prevention involved widespread social distancing, wearing masks, and getting vaccinated, while HIV prevention was less publicized. This was likely due to societal discomfort with openly discussing sex, especially between men, and this has made it difficult to promote preventative methods. However, due to community effort, education about safe sex practices and the use of condoms became key parts of early HIV prevention efforts.

Public messaging about COVID-19 utilized social media, press conferences, and widespread advertising campaigns, facilitating real-time communication and education. Conversely, public information regarding HIV/AIDS initially suffered from silence and misinformation due to cultural discomfort around topics like sexuality and drug use. Eventually, public health advocates like Surgeon General C. Everett Koop played a crucial role in breaking these barriers, promoting frank, fact-based education about HIV transmission and prevention in the late 1980s.[43]

Jonathan Baker, a physician assistant (PA) educator and advocate for healthcare equality in underserved communities, carries this same commitment to dismantling stigma and prioritizing patient trust. He understands that meaningful care starts with making patients feel seen, heard, and valued. During the COVID-19 pandemic, Jonathan didn't just treat patients—he was their advocate, working to bridge the gaps in healthcare access and education. Whether addressing vaccine hesitancy, addressing misinformation, or simply ensuring his patients felt safe in the exam room, he embraced his role as both a provider and a champion for equitable care.

I always try to mirror my patients. Whether their way of dealing with diagnosis is despair, taking action, or being comedic. I meet them where they are. I also make my patients feel comfortable by describing their treatment options. I give them the risks and benefits of each so they can choose for themselves. We discuss how the options will impact various aspects of their lives outside of the exam room. Almost always, they choose the same option I recommend.

At first glance, the HIV/AIDS and COVID-19 pandemics seem like entirely different crises, shaped by

---

[43] Lushniak BD. Surgeon general's perspectives. *Public Health Rep.* 2014 Mar-Apr;129(2):112-4. doi: 10.1177/003335491412900202. PMID: 24587543; PMCID: PMC3904888.

different times, different responses, and different social attitudes. One was met with neglect and stigma, the other with swift medical advancements and global action. But for those who lived through both, the connections run deeper than the differences.

For people with HIV, the COVID-19 pandemic was not just a new health threat—it was a painful reminder of past neglect and, in many ways, an extension of the same fight. Many were at higher risk of severe illness due to compromised immune systems, yet they faced uncertainty about how the virus would affect them and whether their antiretroviral treatments still offered protection. The barriers to care and the fear of being deprioritized in life-saving treatment were all too familiar. As the world scrambled to respond to COVID-19, many people with HIV found themselves facing renewed discrimination, unanswered medical questions, and a lingering sense of invisibility.

But some refused to let history repeat itself. Jonathan became an anchor for his community. He saw firsthand how many of his patients felt abandoned, especially those with HIV—isolated not just by the physical risks of COVID-19, but by the fear that they would be forgotten once again. Instead of treating them as just another high-risk category, Baker made it his mission to ensure that they were heard, understood, and prioritized.

This community had seen this before—the fear, the misinformation, the way the most vulnerable got left behind. During the HIV/AIDS crisis, it was silence that killed. During COVID-19, it was noise—conspiracies, half-truths, and policies that looked good on paper but failed the people who needed them most.

He spent his days doing what he could. Explaining, again and again, that treatment worked, that vaccines mattered, and that his patients weren't forgotten. When vaccines finally became available to non-healthcare related workers, they were offered first to high-risk groups—immunocompromised people, the elderly, those with underlying conditions. On paper, this meant protection. In reality, it often meant long waits, confusion, and difficulty accessing appointments.

I feel honored to care for my community, which is especially affected by HIV. Early in the COVID-19 pandemic, I noticed my patients and friends struggling with feelings reflecting those from the early days of the HIV epidemic. Instead of starting with questions about their physical health, I would begin by asking, "How are you doing?" because many were not doing well. By showing empathy and care, I wanted my patients to know I was there for them and that this situation was different.

He listened when his patients told him they didn't trust the system, when they worried they'd be pushed aside once again. It felt like the world seemed to be moving on without them.

These pandemics were decades apart, but the failures felt familiar. The people most at risk had to fight the hardest for care, the hardest for dignity. The lesson was clear: public health can't just be about medicine. It has to be about people.

Pediatric Obesity on the Rise

Dr. Megan Bensignor is a pediatric endocrinology and obesity medicine specialist. During the pandemic, she noticed her pediatric patients were gaining weight significantly. Schools, gyms, and sporting facilities had shut down, and younger children started adding pounds excessively. This weight gain, like a domino effect, started affecting their physical and mental health.

Dr. Bensignor also noticed that the pandemic shocked children who typically spend most of their day at school with teachers and peers. The lockdown cut off their social connections, halted recreational activities, social gatherings, sports, and isolated them at home. This sudden change resulted in increased stress levels, which likely led to unhealthy eating habits, a sedentary lifestyle, and a disruption of their medication regimens. People needed help to fight these factors. So, Dr. Bensignor and her team helped patients and their families schedule physical activity and medications.

But as they worked hard, evidence emerged showing that children with obesity could have an increased risk of COVID-19 complications.[44] Yet again, Dr. Bensignor and her team educated families on protective measures while still supporting increased physical activity.

---

[44] Iacopetta D, Catalano A, Ceramella J, Pellegrino M, Marra M, Scali E, Sinicropi MS, Aquaro S. The ongoing impact of COVID-19 on pediatric obesity. Pediatr Rep. 2024 Feb 2;16(1):135-150. doi:10.3390/pediatric16010013. PMID: 38391001; PMCID: PMC10885050.

Physical inactivity caused by pandemic-related isolation and quarantine increased the average body mass index (BMI) by up to 0.198, with boys slightly more affected.[45,46] This statistic shows the pandemic had an impact on the obesity rates of the pediatric population. A third study showed that adults' perceptions of hunger increased several times during the day, naturally making people consume more food.[47]

The pandemic left a lasting mark on our health, especially concerning weight and physical activity. Pediatric patients gained weight as stress levels soared. However, it's not just children who were affected. Adults, too, were significantly affected by heightened perceptions of hunger. Combined with a lack of physical activity, these factors drove up BMI across age groups.

Looking ahead, healthcare professionals must proactively educate their patients about the benefits of movement. From daily walks to community fitness programs, every recommendation can help people reclaim their health. However, the solution shouldn't end with patient education. Policymakers and public health leaders should unite and create policies promoting active lifestyles. Examples include designing more walkable cities, funding

---

[45] An R. Projecting the impact of the coronavirus disease-2019 pandemic on childhood obesity in the United States: A microsimulation model. Journal of Sport and Health Science. 2020 Jul;9(4):302–12.

[46] Ferentinou E, Koutelekos I, Pappa D, Manthou P, Dafogianni C. The Impact of the COVID-19 Pandemic on Childhood Obesity: A Review. Cureus. 2023 Sep;15(9):e45470.

[47] Di Renzo L, Gualtieri P, Pivari F, Soldati L, Attinà A, Cinelli G, et al. Eating habits and lifestyle changes during COVID-19 lockdown: an Italian survey. J Transl Med. 2020 Dec;18(1):229.

school-based exercise programs, and increasing access to affordable fitness resources.

If unaddressed, the rise in pediatric obesity during the pandemic could have significant long-term consequences. Studies show that children who develop obesity are far more likely to carry excess weight into adulthood, increasing their risk for chronic illnesses such as type 2 diabetes, hypertension, and heart disease.[48] Beyond physical health, obesity in childhood is strongly linked to mental health challenges, including low self-esteem, depression, and anxiety, which can further reinforce unhealthy behaviors. As these children grow older, they may face greater barriers to maintaining an active lifestyle, particularly if their weight gain has already led to reduced mobility or social stigmatization. Without intervention, healthcare systems will see a growing burden of obesity-related diseases, placing additional strain on medical resources. Addressing this crisis now—through early intervention, lifestyle education, and systemic changes to promote healthier habits—will be essential to preventing a future where an entire generation struggles with the compounding effects of obesity.

As we recover from the pandemic's ripple effects, we must shift gears from reactive to proactive towards a healthier future—one with better mental and physical health.

---

[48] Sahoo K, Sahoo B, Choudhury AK, Sofi NY, Kumar R, Bhadoria AS. Childhood obesity: causes and consequences. J Family Med Prim Care. 2015 Apr-Jun;4(2):187-92. doi: 10.4103/2249-4863.154628. PMID: 25949965; PMCID: PMC4408699.

An Honorable Contribution

Dr. Love Chukwuemeka Anani, an emergency medicine physician and medical director at Tristar Northcrest in Springfield, Tennessee, witnessed firsthand the devastating impact of the COVID-19 pandemic on both patient care and hospital operations. As fear of the virus kept people away from seeking medical attention, daily patient volumes at the hospital plummeted from 70–80 to just 30–40. This drastic decline not only led to financial strain but also forced difficult decisions, including staff reductions. Nurse practitioners (NPs) and physician assistants (PAs) were among the hardest hit, highlighting the ripple effect of the crisis—not just on patients, but on the healthcare workforce itself.

Like other businesses, hospitals depend on the volume of customers to generate income. Patients are our customers who pay fees that ultimately support our families and us.

Physicians were less affected by financial losses than NPs and PAs, which Dr. Anani found disheartening. To support his colleagues, he created a medium to collect funds for NPs and PAs.

Working 120-130 hours pre-COVID and then only 80 hours a month during the pandemic—it was shocking to think this would affect their households. I made sure to lead by example, contribute my stipend as a medical director, and encourage others to donate.

As COVID-19 cases surged in August of 2020, the staff was exhausted and struggled to manage severely ill patients. The reduced workforce meant fewer patients could be admitted, causing frustration among those needing care for non-COVID-19 illnesses. Dr. Anani recalled patients questioning why they couldn't be admitted to empty rooms, to which he had to explain the shortage of nursing staff.

Many of them would see empty rooms in the hospital and ask, why can't you put me in that empty room where there is enough space? As providers and administration, we would have to tell them we did not have a nurse to watch them in the room. At one point, people got frustrated and refused to accept that as a valid excuse.

Imagine working at McDonald's. We need you to make 200 big Macs and keep everyone happy with ten people working. We need 30 people to place that order. The same is applicable in the hospital setting. How can only a few staff members manage such an enormous workload?

It was difficult to manage patients during the pandemic. During one instance, Dr. Anani cared for a young, fit patient in his 30s who was admitted for COVID-19 with dangerously low oxygen saturation. Despite Dr. Anani's best efforts, he struggled to raise the patient's oxygen levels. At the time, many interventions commonly used today were unavailable. For instance, administering albuterol or asthma treatments in a standard room was prohibited due to the risk of spreading the infection. Also, providing the patient with regular oxygen through a nasal cannula was not an option. Dr. Anani had no alternative but to intubate the patient. The patient was initially apprehensive but eventually agreed to the procedure.

I remember him fighting that tube. He kept coughing and trying to move the entire time. Normally, when you're sedated, you're completely unconscious and can't feel anything. Even after giving him medications, he continued to move. What we discovered about COVID-19 patients at that time was that they required astronomical levels of sedation compared to other patients.

This story reminds us that it is impossible to know everything in medicine. Despite the experience, Dr. Anani and many of his co-providers discovered many unsettling facts about COVID-19's physical impact. Even though Dr. Anani did what was medically correct then, he asked himself whether he would have given the same treatment that day. Often, providers have to make tough decisions in their stressed environments.

I wonder if he faced unnecessary trauma or if his medical costs or length of stay were increased because of my actions that day. What I did on that day was medically correct. It was also what was being done across the country. I still questioned whether what I did was right for that patient.

In another instance, Dr. Anani shared the story of a man whom we'll name Rick for privacy, an older African American gentleman who had DJed many large parties in Springfield. Rick came to the hospital looking extremely puzzled and frail after undergoing previous COVID-19 treatment. After running tests, Dr. Anani and his team discovered that Rick had suffered a massive stroke.

Although Rick and his family were nervous, they were incredibly cooperative. When Rick returned for a checkup after treatment, Dr. Anani and his team assured him they would consider every possible diagnosis.

The successful interaction between Dr. Anani and Rick was built on mutual trust. Dr. Anani prioritized his safety, even if it meant transferring him to another hospital with better facilities. Similarly, Rick trusted Dr. Anani because he recognized the exceptional care he provided.

He trusted us enough to come back. We also knew he was hard-working and his family depended on him, so we donated to his GoFundMe campaign, so he would not suffer any financial losses. Whenever I see his family, they tell me he is doing well and express gratitude. They trusted us that day, and I continue to thank them for their calmness and unshakable trust in us.

Watching people die daily filled him with anxiety for his own loved ones. He vividly remembered the heartbreak of being unable to accompany his pregnant wife to a doctor's appointment—his exposure to COVID-19 patients deemed too great a risk.

I would feel guilty going in because I did not want to put anyone's life at risk because of me. I would always wear a mask even inside the house and skip many social gatherings because I did not want anyone to suffer because of me. As a provider, my job is to contribute to people's well-being. If being around my loved ones had caused them to get sick, I would never be able to forgive myself.

While facing the challenges of the pandemic, Dr. Anani shifted his perspective to focus on the bright side. He taught us that we can either be disheartened by setbacks or face them with courage. He also emphasized the importance of open-mindedness toward discoveries. Initially seen as a severe flu, COVID-19 caused unexpected devastation, with more unknowns than known. All the while, providers like Dr. Anani approached patients calmly and instilled hope by doing what was best for them, even at personal and financial costs.

Hospitals have never been just places of healing—they are economic engines, shaped by market forces, government policies, and financial incentives. The modern healthcare system is built on a model where care is a commodity, patients are consumers, and survival depends as much on revenue as it does on medicine. Hospitals must generate income to stay open, competing for funding, managing operational costs, and navigating insurance reimbursements. Like any other industry, when profits shrink, cuts follow.

This isn't new. The structure of healthcare has long been dictated by who pays and who profits. In the United States, where privatized healthcare dominates, hospitals rely on a steady influx of paying patients to keep the doors open. Elective surgeries, routine checkups, and specialized treatments drive revenue, while emergency care—though essential—often operates at a loss. When the pandemic hit, those revenue-generating procedures vanished overnight. Hospitals didn't just face a public health emergency—they faced an economic crisis.

As Dr. Anani points out, hospitals operate on volume. They need a constant flow of patients to stay financially afloat. When COVID-19 shut down routine care, the drop in patient numbers drained hospital budgets. The response was swift—job cuts came fast, and they hit hardest in areas deemed nonessential. While ICU doctors and emergency staff braced for impact, nurse practitioners (NPs) and physician assistants (PAs) saw their hours slashed or their jobs disappear altogether. The healthcare system before COVID-19, was now expected to run with fewer workers, even as the crisis deepened.

Those who remained took on impossible workloads. It felt less like a hospital and more like a fast-food kitchen trying to operate with a skeleton crew. Dr. Anani compared it to "a McDonald's with 10 workers trying to make 200 Big Macs." The numbers didn't add up. Too many patients. Not enough hands.

A 2021 study published in the Online Journal of Issues in Nursing backs up what healthcare workers already knew—burnout wasn't just a possibility, it was inevitable. Nurses, in particular, faced impossible expectations, leading to mass resignations and career shifts. Some left for private practice or telehealth.[49] Others left medicine entirely. The result? A workforce that wasn't just overworked, but actively shrinking.

---

[49] Chan G, Bitton J, Allgeyer R, Elliott D, Hudson L, Moulton Burwell P. The Impact of COVID-19 on the Nursing Workforce: A National Overview. Online J Issues Nurs [Internet]. 2021 May 31;26(2). Available from: https://ojin.nursingworld.org/table-of-contents/volume-26-2021/number-2-may-2021/the-impact-of-covid-19-on-the-nursing-workforce/

But this problem didn't start with COVID-19—it just made it visible. Hospitals have always operated as businesses, and when profit margins are the priority, patient care and worker well-being often suffer. Non-physician staff, despite being the backbone of care, were seen as expendable. Retention strategies were an afterthought. The idea of upskilling staff to handle future crises? Largely ignored.

COVID-19 didn't break healthcare's economic model—it exposed what had been true all along: healthcare operates on the same principles as any other industry, shaped by profit margins and financial risk. In times of crisis, the system doesn't bend to meet the needs of the people—it expects the people to bend to meet the needs of the system.

Now, the question is no longer whether the system needs fixing. It's whether we'll make the changes before the next crisis hits.

Graduating in a Pandemic

Dr. Jenna Hyer, a periodontist specializing in implant, surgical, and sedation dentistry, was two months away from finishing her residency when the pandemic struck. Due to the lockdown, she could not return to the clinic to complete her residency.

Finding a position in periodontics isn't just about skill—it relies heavily on referrals, networking, and building relationships within the dental community. But during COVID-19, those essential connections became nearly impossible to make. The usual dental society events, conferences, and in-person meetings where new professionals could connect with established practitioners were canceled. The very spaces where careers were built no longer existed.

For the most part, I had to drive to every dental office and introduce myself. It takes several meetings for people to know you and trust you enough to start referring others to you. Much of it is door-to-door and meeting people, which was difficult to do during the pandemic.

During these times, dentists feared shutting down their practice. Almost every dentist wished to go back to work and continue serving people. However, many patients wanted to avoid coming to the clinic. Those who came were often anxious.

It is already terrifying for people to be in a dentist's office with a bright light on their faces. Their fear worsened when they saw us wearing PPE and big face shields. I had patients who never saw my face.

Sensing the apprehension among her patients, Dr. Hyer introduced a hybrid format into her practice. She added a virtual connection with her patients, which helped reduce their fears and keep them happy to return for treatment if needed.

Even though she noted fear among her patients, Dr. Hyer said she and her colleagues did not fear COVID-19 much. Many dentists treat every patient as potentially infectious and use precautions to prevent the spread of diseases. They often used air filters, masks, and face shields before the COVID-19 pandemic began.

A 2022 study published in the *Journal of Interprofessional Education & Practice* emphasizes the importance of effective communication and interprofessional collaboration in healthcare, especially during the pandemic.[50] Healthcare workers found that their traditional team structures and communication processes were severely disrupted, particularly as some transitioned to remote work. However, for those who remained in inpatient settings, the pandemic led to an improvement in teamwork by breaking down hierarchies and fostering mutual support among frontline staff.

---

[50] Jordan SR, Connors SC, Mastalerz KA. Frontline healthcare workers' perspectives on interprofessional teamwork during COVID-19. Journal of Interprofessional Education & Practice. 2022 Dec;29:100550.

Both narratives underline the challenges of maintaining professional relationships and communication in a crisis. Dr. Hyer's adaptation to virtual connections with patients mirrors the healthcare workers' reliance on virtual communication during the pandemic. The study illustrates how remote work fractured established communication patterns, while Dr. Hyer's door-to-door approach illustrates how healthcare professionals in other fields had to find creative ways to maintain relationships. In both cases, the need for adaptability and innovative communication became clear.

The Virus Spoke English First

Dr. Christine O'Dea understood one thing deeply: in Latinx culture, community is everything. Families lean on each other, neighbors act as extended family, and social gatherings are an unspoken tradition. Celebrations aren't just about the event—they're about reinforcing bonds, passing down stories, and maintaining a deep-rooted sense of belonging. Sundays mean shared meals. Birthdays bring entire extended families under one roof. Weddings are community events, not just private affairs. To be Latino is to be connected.

But COVID-19 didn't just disrupt life—it shattered the foundation that held this way of life together.

The Latin population in Cincinnati made up just 5% of the city's population, approximately 15,000 people, but they were disproportionately affected by the pandemic.[51] Many worked essential jobs—cleaning office buildings, stocking grocery stores, or assembling products in warehouses—jobs that couldn't be done remotely. There was no "work from home" option. No paid sick leave. No financial cushion if someone in the household got sick. The risk wasn't just about health; it was about survival.

And yet, another silent crisis unfolded in the background—misinformation.

[51] Census Dots. Cincinnati, OH demographics: A map of Cincinnati's population by race [Internet]. Census Dots. Available from: https://www.censusdots.com/race/cincinnati-oh-demographics

Dr. O'Dea, a family medicine physician at the University of Cincinnati, watched as confusion spread faster than the virus itself. Government agencies published updates in English, sometimes in Spanish, but rarely in the Indigenous Guatemalan languages spoken by many of her patients.

Some of our immigrants are not necessarily literate in English. They have low literacy in Spanish, and their first language may be an Indigenous language. So, we partnered with an organization in Guatemala to develop materials in these languages and shared them out in our community.

Without trusted sources of information, rumors took hold. People weren't sure when to seek care, how to quarantine, or if vaccines were safe. Some feared that testing positive would cost them their job. Others weren't sure how the virus spread—if masks worked, if touching groceries was dangerous, if they could be infected just by standing near someone.

There were just a lot of rumors in the community—about how you could catch it, how bad it was, whether you should wear a mask. And because the Latino community in Cincinnati is relatively small, there weren't always a lot of resources tailored specifically to them. People didn't necessarily know where to turn for accurate information.

Dr. O'Dea realized something critical: telling people to be careful wasn't enough if they didn't understand why. The information gap wasn't just a barrier—it was a public health failure.

She refused to let language be the reason people suffered. She partnered with a non-profit in Guatemala to create digital content in multiple Indigenous languages—languages that had been left out of health communications entirely. These weren't just simple translations. They were tailored to the daily realities of Latino immigrant families, walking them through the pandemic in a way that made sense in their lives.

They covered everything:

- How to social distance in crowded living situations?
- The correct way to wear and clean a mask.
- What to do if you're exposed to the virus?
- How to access medical care without insurance?

But even the best resources meant nothing if they didn't reach the people who needed them. That's when Jorge Benedetti entered the picture.

Trust in healthcare isn't just about access—it's about relationships. In Latin culture, people don't rely on government agencies for guidance as much as they do their community. Neighbors, church leaders, store owners, and local figures shape their understanding of what's safe, what's true, and what's best for their families.

O'Dea understood that if she wanted people to listen, she needed a trusted voice from within the community.

That voice was Jorge Benedetti.

Benedetti wasn't a journalist. He wasn't a doctor. He was a Colombian immigrant with a Facebook group of over 5,000 Latino immigrants—a space where people exchanged everything from job leads to news updates. It was a virtual town square, a lifeline for a community that mainstream news often ignored.

I joined his Facebook group with other Spanish-speaking healthcare providers every Saturday. We discussed all the changes made due to the pandemic and answered people's questions. We also talked about the importance of getting tested and staying home if someone contracted the virus. It worked well because it got thousands of views.

Benedetti's page became a public health tool. Through videos, posts, and live discussions, Dr. O'Dea and her team turned social media into a bridge between medicine and the community. It wasn't just about facts—it was about trust.

As Dr. O'Dea spent more time speaking with patients, a troubling pattern emerged: many Latino immigrants avoided COVID-19 testing because they couldn't afford to test positive.

A lot of immigrants didn't want to get tested. If they tested positive, that meant they were out of work for two weeks—and they needed that paycheck.

The pandemic forced an impossible choice: protect yourself and risk financial ruin or keep working and risk exposure.

For many, the choice was clear.

Public health policies focused on social distancing and isolation—but for Latin communities, these measures weren't just difficult; they were devastating.

Tens of people lived in the same household, close to each other. Many of the Latino population I worked with would have social gatherings every weekend because they took pride in maintaining close ties with their family, friends, and neighbors. The fact that they could no longer do that wrecked their way of life.

Physical health was at stake, but so was mental health.

Mental health in our immigrant population is really challenging. If you don't have insurance, it may be really hard to access mental health services. If you don't speak English fluently, finding a therapist who speaks your language is another challenge. And that's all on top of the stress that already comes with immigration—family separation, adjusting to a new culture, economic hardship.

The pandemic took that existing burden and made it heavier.

Loneliness became a second pandemic, and people turned to opioids and alcohol to cope.

I definitely had patients who were using—whether that was alcohol, cocaine, or opioids. It became a big issue during the pandemic. And now, we're seeing the consequences of that.

Dr. O'Dea's efforts weren't just about COVID-19—they were about the future of public health.

A 2001 study on interpreter services found that when language support was provided, healthcare outcomes improved significantly.[52] More patients followed through with preventive care, understood their diagnoses, and adhered to treatment plans.

Her work mirrored these findings. By providing health information in culturally relevant ways, she helped her patients take control of their health.

Her approach illustrates a deeper truth:

Public health must meet people where they are—whether that's in their language, in their communities, or on their Facebook feed.

[52] Jacobs EA, Lauderdale DS, Meltzer D, Shorey JM, Levinson W, Thisted RA. Impact of interpreter services on delivery of health care to limited-English-proficient patients. J Gen Intern Med. 2001 Jul;16(7):468–74.

Summary and Reflection

The experiences detailed across these chapters highlight a crucial truth: pandemics do not simply expose healthcare vulnerabilities—they illuminate long-standing societal inequities, stigmas, and the delicate balance between community trust and systemic response. The narratives surrounding HIV/AIDS and COVID-19 underscore how prejudice and fear significantly shape public health outcomes. Stigma surrounding sexuality and drug use in the 1980s delayed HIV interventions, prolonging suffering and deepening divisions. In contrast, COVID-19 elicited rapid global action, showcasing that unified, proactive approaches, when possible, can significantly mitigate a crisis. Reflecting on these histories prompts us to consider how individuals within communities can advocate more effectively for equitable healthcare access and actively reduce stigma around health conditions in their day-to-day lives.

Despite quicker scientific breakthroughs and global collaboration seen during COVID-19, the pandemic amplified existing disparities. Communities already burdened by socioeconomic disadvantages, limited access to healthcare, and chronic conditions faced disproportionate impacts. Pediatric obesity surged due to disrupted routines and heightened stress, underscoring the need for accessible preventive care and equitable health education. Delays in cancer screenings due to pandemic fears highlighted the intersection of preventive care, mental health, and the caregiver burden borne predominantly by women and marginalized groups. Recognizing these disparities challenges us to question what role education can play in addressing and dismantling such inequities. It also encourages proactive personal actions like advocating for improved access to preventive healthcare services and supporting community-driven health education initiatives.

The narratives of healthcare providers navigating patient hostility, burnout, and moral distress reveal another vital insight: the healthcare workforce itself is vulnerable. These professionals not only bear the responsibility of patient well-being but also the emotional toll of societal fears and frustrations. The violence and abuse experienced by healthcare providers, coupled with inadequate staffing and resource shortages, underscore the need for systemic reform. Supporting healthcare workers through sustainable staffing, mental health resources, and respectful work environments is not optional—it is foundational. On a personal level, we can advocate for policies and practices that prioritize the mental and physical health of healthcare workers, contribute to creating respectful interactions in healthcare settings, and publicly voice support for better conditions for those who care for us.

As we move forward, these collective experiences offer critical lessons for policymakers, healthcare institutions, and communities alike. Investing proactively in equitable healthcare infrastructure, fostering open and inclusive communication, and prioritizing community engagement are essential steps. Future preparedness must involve not only scientific innovation but structural equity, inclusive public health messaging, and a resilient workforce. Each of us can participate daily by challenging biases, educating ourselves and others about healthcare disparities, volunteering with community health initiatives, supporting local organizations that promote equitable care, and actively engaging in public dialogues about health policy.

These stories compel us to reflect deeply on our interconnectedness and collective vulnerability. Only by acknowledging and addressing the root causes of inequity and stigma can we truly strengthen our public health defenses and emerge more resilient and compassionate when—not if—the next health crisis arises.

Discussion Questions

1. How do historical injustices, such as the Tuskegee Syphilis Study and forced sterilizations, continue to shape the mistrust of the healthcare system among marginalized communities, and what concrete measures can be implemented to rebuild that trust?

2. In what ways do socioeconomic and environmental determinants compound healthcare disparities in low-income, indigenous, and minority populations, and how can public policies effectively address these interlinked challenges?

3. Reflecting on the aftermath of COVID-19, how can healthcare systems balance the need for rapid crisis response with the maintenance of routine, preventive care—such as cancer screenings and chronic disease management—to prevent long-term adverse outcomes?

4. Given the increased stress and mental health challenges faced by both patients and providers during the pandemic, what strategies should be prioritized to support the well-being and resilience of the healthcare workforce?

5. How can digital outreach and culturally tailored communication strategies, like those implemented by Dr. O'Dea for non-English-speaking communities, be scaled and adapted to improve

health literacy and access among other marginalized groups?

Part 4: The Role of Public Perception and Misinformation

Navigating a Distrustful Society

Introduction

Every minute, 456,000 tweets are sent on Twitter. 46,740 photos are posted on Instagram.[53] And with 2 billion active users, Facebook remains the world's largest social media platform—more than a quarter of the global population logs in regularly.[54]

Let that sink in.

In the time it took to read that paragraph, 510,000 comments were posted, 293,000 status updates were shared, and more than 300 million photos were uploaded to Facebook today alone. The digital world is relentless, an unfiltered flood of voices, images, and information. And within that tidal wave, fact and fiction blend so seamlessly that distinguishing between the two feels impossible.

But misinformation isn't new. It has been shaping societies for centuries, from whispered rumors in ancient marketplaces to propaganda that fueled wars. What is new is its speed, reach, and the sheer force with which it embeds itself into daily life, fueled largely by social media algorithms designed to amplify sensational content.

[53] Domo Inc. Data never sleeps 5.0 [Internet]. 2017. Available from: https://web-assets.domo.com/blog/wp-content/uploads/2017/07/17_domo_data-never-sleeps-5-01.png

[54] Statista. Most popular social networks worldwide as of January 2024, ranked by number of monthly active users [Internet]. 2024 [cited 2025 Mar 13]. Available from: https://www.statista.com/statistics/272014/global-social-networks-ranked-by-number-of-users/

The rise of social media has transformed the way misinformation spreads. Algorithms prioritize engagement over accuracy, promoting divisive and misleading content because it keeps users clicking, sharing, and arguing. This digital landscape has eroded trust in institutions, experts, and even the concept of objective truth. Misinformation no longer moves slowly through word-of-mouth—it spreads at the speed of a retweet, a share, or a viral video.

Few modern figures have influenced the spread of misinformation as significantly as Donald Trump. His presidency was a turning point, where falsehoods didn't just slip into public discourse—they dominated it. According to The Washington Post's Fact Checker, Trump made over 30,000 false or misleading claims during his first four years in office, an average of more than 20 per day.[55] His rhetoric fueled distrust in the media, scientific institutions, and even democratic processes, demonstrating just how powerful misinformation can be when repeatedly reinforced at the highest levels of power.

But misinformation doesn't just operate on the grand stage of politics. It affects you in deeply personal ways—when your loved ones fall for conspiracy theories, when your community struggles to discern fact from fiction, when fear drives choices that should be made with reason. It shapes decisions about health, influences whether children receive proper medical care, and dictates public policies that affect millions. This book takes you beyond the headlines, into the lives of those who have fought misinformation firsthand and

---

[55] Kessler G. Trump's false or misleading claims total 30,573 over four years. *The Washington Post*. 2021 Jan 24. Available from: https://www.washingtonpost.com/politics/2021/01/24/trumps-false-or-misleading-claims-total-30573-over-four-years/

those who have suffered because of it.

You'll meet a veterinarian who worked tirelessly to correct false beliefs that led to pets being abandoned in panic. You'll hear from medical professionals on the front lines, witnessing patients delay critical care due to misleading claims about COVID-19. You'll see how children—already among the most vulnerable—were left struggling with untreated vision problems because bureaucratic confusion made access to care even harder.

These aren't just stories. They're warnings. They show what happens when lies spread faster than truth, when fear dictates policy, when institutions fail to counteract deception. They show the cost of complacency.

One of the most damaging consequences of misinformation is the way it exacerbates existing inequalities. Communities of color, already underrepresented in the medical profession, often face additional hurdles in seeking care. A long history of systemic racism in healthcare has sown deep distrust, and misinformation only compounds these fears. When medical professionals do not reflect the communities they serve, skepticism grows, making it even harder to dispel myths and ensure equitable access to accurate health information. The consequences are devastating—delayed treatment, preventable deaths, and an ever-widening gap in healthcare outcomes.

Addressing misinformation requires collective effort. Social media platforms must take responsibility, strengthening fact-checking mechanisms and reducing the virality of falsehoods. But individuals, too, have a role to play. Digital literacy, critical thinking, and a willingness to question sources are essential in combating the spread of misinformation. Additionally, increasing representation in the medical field and fostering community-based healthcare initiatives can help rebuild trust and ensure that accurate, culturally competent information reaches those who need it most.

As you read, ask yourself: How much of what you believe has been shaped by misinformation? How often have you second-guessed what's true? And most importantly—what will you do about it? The era of misinformation is here. The only question is whether you will passively absorb it—or fight back.

The Pets Left Behind

The difference between deciphering information online and simply consuming it lies in the ability to critically analyze research, separate facts from misinformation, and assess the credibility of sources. It's not just about reading headlines or following social media trends—it requires actively questioning where the information comes from, understanding the data behind claims, and recognizing biases.

During the COVID-19 pandemic, fear spread faster than facts. Some pet owners, gripped by uncertainty, abandoned their animals, convinced that their furry companions could transmit the virus. The panic escalated after a television program speculated that pets might pose a risk, triggering a wave of unnecessary pet surrenders. Shelters filled overnight. Dogs and cats once considered family were suddenly seen as potential threats.

Dr. Mira Tabet, a veterinarian from Lebanon, refused to let misinformation dictate the fate of these animals. As reports of abandoned pets surged, she stepped forward—not just as a veterinarian, but as an advocate. She worked tirelessly with animal welfare organizations to debunk the myth that pets were a danger to their owners, using every platform available to spread accurate information.

Her work reflected the deeper issue: understanding the difference between misinformation and fact is not passive—it requires effort. People who lacked the ability to decipher credible information fell victim to fear, while those who questioned sources, reviewed scientific research, and sought expert guidance avoided the panic.

Dr. Tabet didn't just fight for animals—she fought for truth. She reminded people that science, not fear, should guide decisions, and that deciphering information correctly can mean the difference between protecting what we love or abandoning it.

You don't have a choice when you see a dog in pain. You must save him even if you haven't slept for days and are completely drained. It's the oath I took as a vet—to help any pet in need—that keeps me going. When I was tired, I'd remind myself that this phase would pass and the pets needed me. I'd tell myself that the pet was suffering more than I was, so I needed to deal with my pain and help them first. Then I could rest later.

Dr. Tabet's efforts began to shift the public perception, leading many to welcome their pets back into their homes once they realized pets were not COVID-19 carriers. She found that while many people sought companionship from pets, they quickly abandoned them at the first sign of perceived danger. She continued her work out of love and responsibility for the animals in pain, often working without breaks, adequate protective equipment, or sufficient staff.

The challenges within healthcare systems, including the veterinary field, often go unnoticed because their impact is not immediately visible to the broader public. Had Dr. Tabet and her peers chosen to remain silent, many more animals would have suffered and needlessly died during the pandemic. Her story is a testament to strength and dignity, as she decided to educate the public and fight against injustices inflicted upon pets, even at significant personal and professional risk.

Dr. Tabet had seen enough fear-fueled decisions to know how dangerous misinformation could be. She watched as animals were abandoned in the streets and as families made heartbreaking choices based not on science, but on the uncertainty that consumed them. She knew these choices weren't made out of cruelty, but out of misplaced fear—fear that could have been prevented with the right information.

The facts were there. They had always been there. Research published in Forensic Science International: Reports confirmed what Dr. Tabet already suspected: the risk was nearly nonexistent. The study concluded, "It should be noted that there are few cases of companion animals contracting COVID-19 and no evidence of transmission back to human owners."[56]

But people needed more than research papers. They needed trusted voices.

The U.S. Centers for Disease Control and Prevention (CDC) weighed in, reaffirming that animals played no significant role in spreading the virus. The agency cited only a handful of cases worldwide where mammalian animals had transmitted COVID-19 to humans—farmed mink in Europe and the United States, white-tailed deer in Canada, pet

[56] Parry NMA. COVID-19 and pets: When pandemic meets panic. Forensic Science International: Reports. 2020 Dec;2:100090.

hamsters in Hong Kong, and a single cat in Thailand.[57] In nearly every case, the animals were first infected by humans, not the other way around.

The numbers were clear: pets were not the enemy. But in a world consumed by uncertainty, clarity wasn't always enough.

This was more than just a public health issue—it was a test of how we, as a society, handle fear. When faced with the unknown, do we act with compassion, or do we discard what no longer feels safe? How easily do we let go of the things we love when panic creeps in?

Dr. Tabet wasn't just working to protect animals—she was working to restore trust. Trust in science, in rationality, in the bonds between people and their pets. She wasn't naïve; she knew that fear wasn't easily undone. But she also knew that fear didn't have to win.

The data, the research, the official statements—all of it pointed to the same conclusion: the risk was minimal, and the real harm was being done not by the animals, but by the choices people made out of fear.

If anything needed to be contained, it wasn't pets—it was misinformation.

[57] The Centers for Disease Control and Prevention (CDC). Animals and COVID-19 [Internet]. Available from: https://www.cdc.gov/coronavirus/2019-ncov/daily-life-coping/animals.html.

Blurry Vision

We often focus on the impact COVID-19 had on our hospitals, the job market, and the shortage of workers. While that is important, we must also discuss what our children experienced. During the pandemic, our children struggled with several issues, such as being deprived of their typical education, recreational activities, and social interactions. To highlight some of these struggles, Dr. Allegra Burgher, a pediatric optometrist, highlighted the impact of COVID-19 on her young patients.

During COVID-19, I saw students who could not see clearly and needed glasses. I also saw patients with severe eye infections. Some patients with infections chose not to come in for treatment because they hoped the infection would heal on its own and did not want to catch the virus. When they came in, we needed to help them immediately.

This hesitation shown above, delayed appropriate care for blurred vision, strabismus, infections, and other eye complaints. The postponement of care impacted the children's academic and social activities and, in some cases, affected the normal development of vision. To further complicate access to care, many specialists reduced their hours or shut down their clinics altogether. Since families were already scared to come into the clinic, and some clinics were no longer open, finding an appointment became much more difficult.

Alongside delays in seeking care, children also suffered from blurry vision due to delays in making and delivering glasses for patients with Medi-Cal, a state-funded health system in California, like most states' Medicaid programs. This delay often occurred when there was a COVID-19 outbreak in the lab responsible for fabricating eyewear for children with Medi-Cal, causing the lab to shut down for 14 days. These outbreaks occurred often as the virus spread rapidly throughout California. With each new outbreak, the lab paused all orders for glasses until it completed a two-week lab quarantine. This delay prevented children from receiving their glasses for about three to four months after placing their order.

Due to contracts with the state insurance plan, physicians could not order glasses from a different lab if Medi-Cal was covering them. Having Medi-Cal insurance in 2020 meant that these families were at or up to 266% of the federal poverty level.[58] Therefore, the children whose glasses were significantly delayed were those with the most economic disadvantages. Some families paid out of pocket to use a non-Medi-Cal glasses lab, and we offered significant discounts to provide that option to those families. This delay occurred throughout California, and several lobbyists and doctors came together to find a solution but were unsuccessful.

Some kids received their glasses in four weeks, while others waited months at a time. These were kids who had such strong prescriptions and no glasses that it was certain they were not doing well in their school activities. It broke my heart.

---

[58] DB101 California. Medi-Cal: Overview [Internet]. Available from: https://ca.db101.org/ca/programs/health_coverage/medi_cal/program2a.htm

In addition to these difficulties, Dr. Burgher used telemedicine to determine whether patients needed an in-person visit and address concerns about coming into the clinic. The team used a HIPAA-compliant app that allowed patients to send pictures of their eyes, allowing the health providers to evaluate their condition. They used telehealth for red-eye conditions and vision therapy. Although they had high expectations from the app, its functionality fell short. The main problem with the app was that it was complicated and not intuitive. It was challenging to log in, find your doctor, set up an appointment, pre-pay, and be online at the right time.

Fortunately, physicians completed the vision therapy aspect of the clinical service through telehealth and Zoom. The telehealth vision therapy included eye exercises, lenses, equipment, and coaching methods to treat various eye problems. The doctors at her clinic, including Dr. Burgher, also mailed packets with the needed equipment for the vision therapy that week or set up a "drive-by pick-up" for patients' homework and teletherapy visits.

During this time, especially in the early days of COVID-19, people were unsure how the virus was spreading. Some studies suggested that COVID-19 can be transmitted through ocular secretions and tears, putting many eye care specialists at increased risk of contracting the virus. So, trying to protect herself, Dr. Burgher kept a separate paper bag at work for each day, in which she quarantined all of her clothes in her office and only brought them home after leaving them for one week. She and her colleagues also tried to get protective supplies to protect themselves from the virus but could not always source the correct materials. No one could buy disposable masks because manufacturers delivered them to local hospitals. The clinic requested that all doctors wear N-95 masks instead, but it took several months to get just one.

Thankfully, their patients brought them hand-made masks as support. This kindness from patients helped bring energy to the staff and reinvigorated them. Dr. Burgher's mentor, who also practiced in the same clinic, provided thoughtful messages each week, which helped keep spirits high. These combined efforts contributed to giving the best care to the children.

Reflecting on these struggles, Dr. Burgher saw how COVID-19 helped providers triage urgent eye problems with a televisit. She also highlighted several flaws in the Medi-Cal system that directly impacted kids of the lowest socioeconomic class. Hearing this and the news about the virus, she was afraid about bringing the virus to her immunocompromised patients unknowingly. That fear affected her social life, as she constantly worried about what she might bring to work. As a result, Dr. Burgher limited her social circle to her family. She strived through these struggles and could not have supported her patients without the generosity of kind parents who provided PPE and kind words from her mentors and coworkers. We thank her for her outstanding efforts to care for the children's eyes in such fearful circumstances

The Cost of Caution

During the pandemic, Dr. Karl Golnik, a neuro-ophthalmologist and chairman at the University of Cincinnati, juggled more responsibilities than he anticipated. His job was to manage a hospital and university alongside guiding future medical professionals. As a professor and chairman, he supported student residents who were deeply anxious about their future as physicians. Many of these residents feared their ability to perform surgical procedures correctly due to cancellations caused by the pandemic, along with the daunting idea of treating critically ill patients in intensive care without prior experience.

While guiding the residents, Dr. Golnik found that many patients were reluctant to seek treatment, even for severe vision conditions, because they feared contracting the virus. Their reluctance was not uncommon but seen widely by medical providers across various specialties, and understandably so. As a neuro-ophthalmologist, Dr. Golnik frequently saw patients with conditions such as brain tumors and strokes and patients whose subtle symptoms of these conditions often led patients to delay seeking treatment.

I encountered patients experiencing double vision. Some had tumors exerting pressure on specific structures, causing double vision, yet they didn't perceive it as a serious issue. Some would close one eye, restoring normal vision, leading them to downplay the seriousness of their condition.

While double vision, or diplopia, can sometimes be temporary and reversible, it can also indicate underlying cranial nerve issues or stroke. It can cause blurred vision, eye pain, and difficulty performing routine tasks like driving and walking.

Many patients hesitated to undergo surgical procedures, so many elective surgeries were canceled, plunging hospitals into financial turmoil. Since elective surgeries yield great revenue for hospitals, this caused a financial strain and led to employee pay cuts. Eventually, technicians and nurses began to resign. Many deemed the risk of infection not worth the compensation they received.

During the pandemic, we had around 700 open positions for nurses and technicians and needed more staff to perform surgeries. The situation becomes much more serious when we cannot admit patients due to bed shortages, forcing us to close the ER.

Despite facing many challenges, Dr. Golnik persevered through the tough times, using the best available resources. He also showed the importance of maintaining composure in stressful situations. Although the pandemic brought uncertainty and chaos, Dr. Golnik's resilience shows that optimism and hope for better days can prevail even in the darkest times.

Dr. Golnik was not only managing his own medical responsibilities but also serving as a mentor to students facing anxiety and uncertainty about their future in medicine. His residents feared their abilities as physicians due to delayed surgical training and the prospect of having to treat critically ill patients without sufficient hands-on experience. This sense of uncertainty was compounded by fears of infection and the lack of clear guidance on how to manage COVID-19 cases.

A 2020 study on the impact of COVID-19 on medical education found that many medical students faced mental health challenges, including anxiety and depression, due to disruptions in their education.[59] A significant number of students struggled with the suspension of clinical rotations and online learning limitations. With online education taking precedence, students were unsure whether virtual platforms could adequately prepare them for hands-on clinical practice, which led to feelings of doubt and fear about their training and future in medicine.

Both Dr. Golnik's residents and the medical students in the study were dealing with the psychological burden of uncertainty. For residents, the anxiety stemmed from the disruption in their surgical education, while for medical students, the shift to online learning and virtual rotations created uncertainty about their competence and preparedness for clinical practice.

To prevent educational disruptions, healthcare institutions must implement proactive solutions. Telemedicine should be strengthened as a reliable alternative for initial consultations, ensuring patients receive timely medical guidance without unnecessary exposure. Public health campaigns should emphasize the importance of seeking care for urgent conditions, reducing the fear that prevented many from seeking help during the pandemic. For

---

[59] Alsoufi A, Alsuyihili A, Msherghi A, Elhadi A, Atiyah H, Ashini A, et al. Impact of the COVID-19 pandemic on medical education: Medical students' knowledge, attitudes, and practices regarding electronic learning. PLoS One. 2020;15(11):e0242905.

medical education, hybrid models that incorporate virtual learning alongside in-person training can prepare future physicians more effectively. Simulation-based training, for example, can supplement lost hands-on experiences. Additionally, wellness programs should be integrated into medical training to help students manage stress and uncertainty during crises.

Choosing Our Words Carefully

Before conversing with a patient who is against receiving the vaccine, you must assess your mental state as a provider. Your attitude and feelings influence conversations. What were your experiences like before that interaction? Was this your tenth conversation about vaccine hesitancy on the same day?

Dr. Kristina Krohn, an internal medicine and pediatric hospitalist and an assistant professor at the University of Minnesota, sought ways to educate medical students on identifying authentic vs. misleading pandemic information in mass media, conveying information about the pandemic to marginalized populations, and informing patients about the vaccine.

Dr. Krohn's elective course, "COVID-19: Outbreaks and the Media," stressed the importance of future medical providers communicating with patients in simple, understandable terms. While medical providers are trained to speak in medical terminology with their peers, this jargon can be confusing and lead to patient miscommunication. To effectively educate patients, it's essential to use language they can easily grasp and relate to.

When a patient doesn't believe in COVID-19 but shows symptoms like difficulty breathing, I focus on addressing their specific issues. For instance, if they're struggling to breathe, I concentrate on finding ways to help with that symptom. I might explain that while their difficulty breathing could be related to COVID-19, our main goal is to ease their breathing problems. By focusing on their symptoms, I can have more productive conversations with them.

To help these patients, we can use our words to relieve their concerns and give them ease. We can ask them what we can give them to comfort them. During the pandemic, patients sometimes found it difficult to identify authentic versus inauthentic information among the various types of information they were exposed to. Their understanding of the pandemic was influenced by the fear caused by increased sickness and death rates.

Since some patients do not completely trust the healthcare system, it's our responsibility as healthcare providers to bridge this gap. We can do so by educating patients about the pandemic and its effects on their health. This will help us earn their trust, establish meaningful relationships, and allow patients to feel comfortable enough to share their fears and concerns.

Dr. Krohn emphasized the need for clear communication and simplifying medical language to ensure patients understand the information and feel empowered to make informed decisions. Supporting Dr. Krohn's idea, a 2010 study in the *Journal of Nursing Administration* showed that the absence of effective communication between patients and providers can lead to medical errors and poorer outcomes.[60] The study suggests that providers should assess patient communication needs during routine care to meet the needs of communication-vulnerable patients. The study calls

[60] Patak L, Wilson-Stronks A, Costello J, Kleinpell RM, Henneman EA, Person C, et al. Improving Patient-Provider Communication: A Call to Action. JONA: The Journal of Nursing Administration. 2009 Sep;39(9):372–6.

for a more standardized method for assessing communication needs, particularly for patients with language barriers, non-verbal patients, or those with physical disabilities. This ties into Dr. Krohn's work, where she focuses on marginalized populations, particularly when it comes to understanding the effects of misinformation during the pandemic. For these patients, understanding their symptoms and tailoring conversations to their needs becomes a key step in building trust.

Additionally, Dr. Krohn advocates for a proactive approach, advising medical providers to assess their mental state before engaging with patients who may be difficult or hesitant. Providers should be more mindful of their biases and the external factors that might shape their patient interactions. She encourages providers to reflect on their emotional state before engaging in difficult conversations about vaccine hesitancy, recognizing that we show up better for our patients when we know the emotional state we are coming from.

Uncertainty

I signed up to become a doctor, so working during the pandemic was an obligation for me. But, my husband didn't choose this profession, so I was worried about him getting sick. He has terrible asthma and was among the high-risk groups for contracting COVID-19.

Although difficult to accept, uncertainty is an inevitable part of life. We wish to have control over our lives and feel a sense of security and safety. When events do not go according to plan, our fear may overpower our ability to think and function, as many of us experienced during this pandemic. The coronavirus pandemic demonstrated that life can change instantaneously. It has shown us that nothing in life is constant, and somehow, we need to adapt to change.

When COVID-19 emerged, many unknowns arose, such as how the virus is transmitted, whether it is airborne or present on surfaces and in food, its mortality rate, and the severity of its long-term effects. Yet Dr. Olivia Campa, a general internist at UC Davis Health, and her team tried their best to fight this virus by increasing the resources in their hospital and accommodating as many patients as possible.

Dr. Campa was part of her hospital's COVID-19 response task force. One of their first tasks was to maximize the hospital's capacity. The second task was to optimize its workforce. Although it was relatively easy to prepare more beds for patients, increasing the number of doctors to support them was a challenge. Essentially, they shifted from a care delivery model to a mass delivery model, prompting their workers to care for many more sick patients than usual. One vital step was to shift many subspecialists into generalist roles. This system requires great effort from the physicians and leadership team to determine who can care for critically ill patients in the intensive care unit.

If you force people to do something uncomfortable, they may not do it well. They would work under extreme stress, which could be dangerous for the patients. So, we asked volunteers to work in the ICU.

Additionally, COVID-19 changed much of the healthcare system in just a short time. One example is through the use of telehealth. Initially, people expressed hesitancy and discomfort about doing things differently than before, but they were willing to do anything to ensure their safety and those around them. Everyone made an immense effort to learn and help one another adapt to the technology.

The coronavirus challenged my peers and me in ways we have not been challenged before. We had to teach people how to use new software. Thankfully, there was an IT department trying to help everyone. Also, we had to take responsibility as doctors to support and encourage each other to learn. Everybody took care of patients while also setting up telehealth systems.

The new implementation of telehealth worked wonderfully for many specialties and was a great way to care for patients. Unfortunately, it was not always ideal. Once, Dr. Campa had a patient who complained of shortness of breath. She had him tested for COVID-19, which was negative and prescribed a chest X-ray, a standard procedure that has to be done in person. When he came in, she heard a murmur in his chest and diagnosed him with severe aortic stenosis. Aortic stenosis occurs when a valve in the heart narrows, reducing blood flow into the aorta, an artery that supplies the body with blood. Due to COVID-19, his diagnosis had been delayed by a month.

Unfortunately, due to the constraints of telemedicine, we only know how many conditions went undiagnosed after it was too late and how many patients were misdiagnosed. Despite the difficulties, Dr. Campa and her team did a fantastic job caring for their patients. We applaud her and all those who contributed to helping one another during the pandemic for their efforts.

Summary and Reflection

Misinformation does not operate in isolation; it embeds itself into the structures of society, influencing policies, public behavior, and even the ways we navigate crises. These chapters reveal how falsehoods, whether deliberate or incidental, shape realities—determining who gets access to healthcare, who is left behind, and who ultimately suffers the consequences of unchecked deception.

The modern explosion of misinformation is not an accident. It is the byproduct of systems designed to prioritize engagement over accuracy, profit over public good. The introduction traces this trajectory, emphasizing how digital spaces have accelerated the spread of misinformation to great levels. What was once confined to fringe publications or political pamphlets is now algorithmically amplified, reaching millions within seconds. Donald Trump's presidency is an example of just how powerful misinformation could be when wielded by someone with influence. More than 30,000 false claims recorded in four years—and with each repetition, a new wave of doubt and division.

The real cost of misinformation, however, is not measured in numbers but in lives. A veterinarian battling the hysteria that led to abandoned pets. An eye doctor witnessing children struggle for months without the glasses they needed to see the world clearly. A neuro-ophthalmologist confronting the grim reality of patients delaying care for strokes and brain tumors out of fear. These stories are not anomalies; they are reflections of a broader pattern in which uncertainty and mistrust override reason, leaving communities vulnerable to preventable harm.

What makes misinformation particularly insidious is its ability to prey on preexisting inequalities. Misinformation does not affect all groups equally—it deepens divides, exploiting historical distrust in institutions, particularly within communities of color and low-income populations. The book reveals how systemic failures and bureaucratic red tape, combined with misinformation, create an almost impenetrable barrier to care. Delays in treatment for Medi-Cal patients, vaccine hesitancy, and the disproportionate burden of the pandemic on marginalized groups—all point to a need for solutions that go beyond fact-checking.

The implications for future pandemics are clear. If misinformation could thrive so effectively during COVID-19, despite access to real-time data and expert guidance, what happens when the next global health crisis arrives? With social media's reach only expanding, the infrastructure for misinformation has already been built. Combatting it requires more than reactive measures—it demands systemic change. Social media platforms must be held accountable for their role in spreading misinformation, integrating stricter fact-checking and transparency policies. Governments must recognize misinformation as a public health threat, investing in education and digital literacy initiatives. And perhaps most critically, healthcare systems must engage directly with communities, rebuilding trust through representation and accessibility.

As a society, we must ask ourselves: Have we learned from the past, or are we doomed to repeat it? Because the next crisis is not a matter of if, but when. The question is whether we will meet it prepared or let misinformation dictate its course.

Discussion Questions

1. As misinformation becomes more deeply embedded in digital spaces, what ethical responsibilities should technology companies bear in addressing its spread?

2. How did the COVID-19 pandemic expose weaknesses in public health communication, and what reforms could prevent similar failures in the future?

3. What strategies can be employed to combat misinformation within communities that have historically distrusted institutions?

4. How does misinformation intersect with issues of economic and racial inequality, and what are the long-term consequences of these disparities?

5. Looking ahead, what policies and public initiatives could help strengthen resilience against misinformation before the next global health crisis?

Part 5: The Evolving Role of Healthcare Education

Medical Training and Learning in Crisis

Introduction

In medicine, the stakes have always been life and death. Hospitals overflow with patients in crisis—some suffering from acute illnesses, others bearing the cumulative toll of long-term neglect—while a new generation of medical professionals struggles under unprecedented pressures. The traditional methods of training doctors and nurses, with neatly compartmentalized lectures and clinical rotations, once appeared sufficient. However, when a global pandemic upended every assumption about access to care, delivery methods, and the very essence of "good medicine," it also exposed the limitations of standard protocols in adapting to a rapidly changing reality.

Medical education, at its core, was never meant to stand still. It was built to respond to the unknown, to prepare hearts and minds for the unpredictability of the next patient, the next pathogen, the next societal shift. Yet the crisis we've endured—and continue to endure—has exposed how unprepared even the best-prepared can be. Lectures on physiology and pharmacology only scratch the surface; the most profound lessons come when you're faced with rooms packed beyond capacity or when misleading headlines and frantic social media posts undermine what you've been taught. The field has grown more complicated and more urgent, demanding a kind of readiness that can't always be found in textbooks.

Still, despite all the changes, the heart of medicine remains a promise: to heal, to protect, to serve. That promise stands even when the system feels rigged against both providers and patients—when training demands all your waking hours, when misinformation poisons public trust, when disparities in access and care weave injustice into daily practice. The stories that follow are about that promise under siege. They show what happens when bright, compassionate people collide with a system that's simultaneously evolving and cracking under pressure.

Today's educators, seasoned practitioners, and new trainees alike wrestle with a pressing question: How do we ready tomorrow's healers for a constantly shifting world? The pandemic was a wake-up call that our teaching and learning strategies must be as dynamic as the crises we face. We need healthcare education that braces for tragedy before it strikes, that confronts bias in every ward and every policy, that empowers professionals to treat whole communities—not just symptoms—and that helps them keep faith in the oath they swore when everything around them suggests giving up.

This moment offers a chance to reinvent how we shape the healers of tomorrow. From the smallest clinics to the largest research hospitals, every story echoes the same refrain: We cannot return to the way things were. The accounts in these pages show us what can happen when we look beyond standard checklists of competencies and recalibrate our sense of what medical education must accomplish. In doing so, new mediums emerge—programs like Pre-Health Shadowing, for instance, open virtual doors that once felt locked, providing students of every background a chance to connect and engage with healthcare professionals. Such novel approaches can break down geographic, financial, and cultural barriers, allowing more aspiring professionals than ever to experience what medicine entails before they even step foot in a hospital corridor.

They remind us, too, that training doctors isn't merely about imparting facts and skills—it's about forging resilience, compassion, and integrity in a chaotic, ever-changing world. Every chapter ahead holds a piece of that puzzle, demonstrating why rethinking how we teach healthcare matters more than ever. Because in the end, the future of healthcare hinges not on the gloss of our buildings or the flash of our technology, but on the people we're guiding into the field—and how we prepare them to meet a crisis head-on with courage, skill, and a determination to heal not just bodies, but a wounded system itself.

Walking Against the Wind

Amid significant overwhelm and mounting responsibilities, Dr. Kerri M. Lockhart made the difficult decision to step away from clinical medicine. Coincidentally, this was when the world navigated one of the deadliest pandemics in history. In the earliest days of the pandemic, guidance on COVID-19 prevention was inconsistent. Health authorities reported that masks were not necessary to prevent transmission—a recommendation that would later prove dangerously incorrect. Trusting this guidance but still apprehensive, Dr. Lockhart continued to work unmasked. That decision led to becoming sick. She became among the first few hundred people to contract COVID-19 in Chicago.

Because of her long history of asthma, Dr. Lockhart initially attributed her early symptoms—breathlessness, a dry cough, and an asthma flare-up—to her preexisting condition rather than COVID-19. As a result, she continued seeing patients for two to three days. However, growing concerns about her asthma and the potential risks of contracting COVID-19 led her to reconsider her decision not to wear a mask. By coincidence, she chose to start wearing one on the same day her symptoms first appeared. She believes this precautionary step played a crucial role in greatly preventing the spread of the virus to her patients while allowing her to continue providing care.

Eventually, Dr. Lockhart's breathing worsened fast. A deep, aching tightness settled in her chest, her breath coming in shallow gasps. She picked up the phone, dialling her

PCP's office with trembling fingers. The clinic squeezed her in for an emergency appointment. A presumptive COVID-19 diagnosis. Three days later, the test confirmed what she already suspected—COVID-19, pneumonia, and an acute asthma flare-up.

The fever came next, creeping in slowly. Her head throbbed, a constant pounding that no amount of water or rest could ease. The coughing wouldn't stop. By the fourth day, she was drenched in sweat, her body wracked with chills, lungs burning with every inhale. It was early in the pandemic. No antivirals, no proven treatments—just guesswork and symptom management. The doctor prescribed an antibiotic for pneumonia, albuterol and oral steroids to open her airways, antipyretics for the fever. She swallowed each pill and hoped for the best.

During the most challenging days of her illness, Dr. Lockhart miserably longed for her fever to subside, her breathing to become less strenuous, and the heaviness in her chest to lift. There was an odd comfort in falling sick so early. She hadn't yet seen the steady stream of names and faces lost to the virus, the headlines filled with rising death tolls. But that same timing left her stranded in uncertainty. No clear guidelines. No treatment protocols. No way to know when—or if—she was out of danger.

Fear crept in. Just enough to make her ask her sister and brother-in-law to check in on her. They did more than that. They set up an old baby monitor in her room, listening for every breath, every shift under the covers. Nights were the hardest. She could feel their worry from the next room.

The recovery dragged on. Three weeks at home before she could even think about work. A month on steroids just to breathe a little easier. Eight to ten weeks before she could move without exhaustion pressing down on her. Nearly six months before she felt something close to normal again.

While recovering at home, she felt an immense emotional burden of guilt for being away from the office and unable to support her physician colleagues during a tough time. Dr. Lockhart found connecting with physicians across the U.S. beyond uplifting, and she missed that. It allowed her to share insights, learn from their experiences, and stay abreast of the ever-changing information about COVID-19. In this way, she felt connected to the goal of keeping as many people alive and healthy as possible.

Reflecting on this period in her life, she recalled the early days of the pandemic and her struggle to process each new piece of information about COVID-19. She remembered a news briefing from when the virus had yet to be detected in the U.S.:

"When the virus arrives, expect significant disruption to your everyday lives."

The speaker repeated and emphasized the phrase—"significant disruption to your everyday lives"—a warning that lodged itself in my mind.

Perplexed by those words, she felt a pang of anxiety in her stomach. Like many, she hoped that, at worst, the crisis would be manageable with the proper preparations made by our leaders monitoring COVID-19 across the globe, and at best, by the time it reached U.S. shores, the spread would have slowed down. Dr. Lockhart found it challenging to imagine how she, a young and healthy person with well-controlled asthma—without the need for a controller or regular use of her rescue inhaler—could become severely ill from this virus. The many warnings associated with COVID-19 were unprecedented compared to any virus she had encountered before, leaving her unsure of how concerned she needed to be. So, when COVID-19 reached the U.S., it became clear that the virus had not slowed, and the preparations in place were no match for its impact.

Being young and healthy did little to ease Dr. Lockhart's fears. Social media turned into a running obituary, each day bringing news of acquaintances' loved ones or distant colleagues lost to the virus.

Social media was also flooded with false claims: the vaccine altered DNA, caused infertility, or was rushed and unsafe. She saw these concerns reflected in her own circles—patients, friends, even family members were hesitant.

But words weren't enough. People needed to see it. When the vaccine became available, she recorded herself getting the shot, explaining why she trusted it. Then, she did something even more impactful: she documented the days that followed. Every day, she posted updates on how she felt, addressing common concerns about side effects.

The response was immediate.

"I wasn't sure, but seeing you do this made me feel safe."

"Your updates helped me decide—I got my shot today."

"Thank you for being honest. This gave me the confidence to move forward."

Her transparency mattered. It built trust in a way statistics and public health statements never could.

Dr. Lockhart was moved that her transparency and genuine concern prevented someone from succumbing to COVID-19. Dr. Lockhart was happy, but to her dismay, moments like these were much more infrequent than she had anticipated. And it would ultimately contribute to her departure.

The stress of practicing medicine during the COVID-19 pandemic certainly played a role in Dr. Lockhart's decision to step away, but the pressure had been building long before the crisis began. Medicine had always demanded more from her—not just in hours or effort, but in the extra, unseen work she had to put in to keep up.

From an early age, she was high-achieving, ambitious, and deeply committed to her education. She attended boarding school for gifted students, then pushed through college, medical school, and residency, excelling at every stage—but always at a cost. Late nights, exhaustive note-taking, double and triple-checking her work—whatever it took, she did it.

Residency tested her in ways she hadn't expected. When she was diagnosed with breast cancer, she convinced herself she could handle it. She kept going through treatment, through fatigue, through stress. Hard work had always been the answer, and she believed if she just pushed harder, she would get through it.

Then came the pediatric board exam. She failed. She told herself it was because she hadn't had enough time to study. But when she failed again—despite studying as much as possible—doubt crept in. Why was it that no matter how hard she worked, it still felt like she was barely keeping up?

A follow-up visit with her oncologist led to an unexpected suggestion: an evaluation for ADHD. Testing confirmed what she had unknowingly been managing her entire life. Suddenly, everything made sense—the constant need for extra effort, the exhaustion, the strategies she had unknowingly built to compensate. Dr. Lockhart, like many women with ADHD, wasn't diagnosed until later in life because her symptoms didn't fit the traditional, male-centered model of hyperactivity and impulsivity. Instead of being disruptive, she had learned to mask her struggles with discipline and hard work, pushing through medical school and residency without realizing that the constant exhaustion and effort to stay organized were signs of an underlying condition.

Upon receiving an explanation for her challenges, Dr. Lockhart's relief was equal to her disappointment in recognizing that the space yet to be created for physicians like her, whose brains work differently, did not exist. While simultaneously contending with the shame that can accompany a diagnosis like this while being a physician, she had a realization that the healthcare field still struggles to include those who are neurodivergent. In her experience, people see neurodivergence as a character flaw and a matter of willpower.

Estimates suggest that 15% to 20% of the global population is neurodivergent, encompassing a wide range of brain differences such as autism, ADHD, dyslexia, and dyspraxia.[61] Neurodiversity recognizes that these variations are not necessarily deficits but natural differences in how brains function, process information, and engage with the world. Autism spectrum conditions involve differences in social interaction, communication, and sensory processing, while ADHD is characterized by challenges with attention, hyperactivity, and impulsivity. Dyslexia primarily affects reading and spelling, and dyspraxia impacts motor skills and coordination. Despite these differences, neurodivergent individuals bring unique strengths—such as creativity, deep focus, and problem-solving—that can enrich any field, including medicine. Yet, the healthcare system often fails to support them, placing barriers in their path instead of leveraging their strengths.

Neurodivergent doctors—including those with ADHD, autism, dyslexia, and other cognitive differences—have always been part of the medical workforce, yet historically many felt pressure to hide their neurodiversity due to stigma. In fear of judgment around her diagnosis, Dr. Lockhart hesitated to ask for support, fearing it would only lead to scrutiny or unfavorable consequences. Instead, she chose to manage it on her own, relying on the same coping

[61] Doyle N. Neurodiversity at work: a biopsychosocial model and the impact on working adults. *Br Med Bull.* 2020 Oct 14;135(1):108-125. doi: 10.1093/bmb/ldaa021. PMID: 32996572; PMCID: PMC7732033.

mechanisms that had carried her through years of rigorous training.

But the weight of it all began to settle in. Was she really helping herself—or just reinforcing the idea that she had to struggle in silence? She found herself questioning the very advice she gave to her patients:

How can I explain encouraging my patients to ask for support when I am knowingly not asking for the support I need and deserve?

Dr. Lockhart knew what it meant to push through. She had done it her whole life—through medical school, through residency, through breast cancer. But medicine wasn't built for doctors like her, and it showed in the smallest ways.

Charting had always been a struggle. Too many details, too many distractions, too much pressure to finish fast. She knew what she needed: structured time, small adjustments, a system that worked with her brain instead of against it. She asked for it, over and over. Denied.

For years, she managed, piecing together her own solutions, working harder to make up for what the system refused to provide. Then, finally—a small win. They approved her request. With that single accommodation, she thrived. Notes closed on time, stress levels down. She could breathe.

Then, just as easily, it was gone. No explanation. No discussion. Just a return to the way things had always been. She asked again. Denied. Again. Denied.

She was done being surprised. Medicine could change overnight for a pandemic but couldn't bend an inch for her. Barriers instead of bridges. Criticism instead of compassion. Exclusion instead of belonging.

And still, she showed up. For her patients, for her colleagues, for the work she had dedicated her life to. But even the most resilient among us have a breaking point.

Nearly ten years of walking against the wind. Ten years of trying to belong in a place that kept telling her she didn't.

I began to develop some clarity about my long-term path. I knew that making an impact in my community was of utmost importance to me. Doing this while simultaneously protecting my physical and mental health was equally important. It was becoming clear that, at the time, healthcare felt unwelcoming to me; someone who, despite being an excellent doctor, would continue to struggle because my challenges did not align with what was considered acceptable. So, if I was to protect my well-being and serve my community, I did not see a path to doing that inside the walls of healthcare at that time. And that broke my heart immensely.

Dr. Lockhart couldn't ignore the contradiction. During the COVID-19 pandemic, healthcare adapted at a lightning fast pace—new treatments, innovative technologies, entire hospital wings restructured in record time to meet the crisis. The urgency of the moment demanded swift action. Yet, when it came to inclusion—ensuring that neurodivergent physicians and others with diverse needs had the support to thrive—the system remained rigid. Progress stalled.

Hesitation replaced urgency. Despite its ability to evolve under immense pressure, healthcare struggled to extend that same adaptability to the people within it.

She had spent years proving she belonged, fighting for space, for understanding, for accommodations that would let her do what she did best: care for patients. But medicine had its limits. And she had reached hers.

Leaving wasn't easy. The guilt clung to her. Her patients, their families—she had built relationships, earned their trust. Walking away felt like abandoning them. But staying meant abandoning herself.

The fear was there, too. First, the fear of not knowing—of struggling through medical training without understanding why her brain worked differently. Then, the fear of knowing—of naming it, of asking for support in a system that wasn't built to give it. Even now, as conversations around equity and inclusion grew louder, neurodivergent doctors were still expected to fit into a system that refused to fit them.

She had spent her career trying to make it work. Now, she had to face the hardest truth of all: it wasn't her that needed fixing.

Dr. Lockhart's story exposes a hard truth: the healthcare system can move fast when it wants to. She wasn't alone in this struggle. Fewer than 40% of medical schools reported offering clinical accommodations,[62] their support stopping at written exams and lectures but rarely extending into rotations or patient care. Neurodivergent students learned to navigate a world that wasn't built for them, working twice as hard just to keep up. Despite legal protections, cultural and administrative barriers persist. Dr. Lockhart knew firsthand how high-stakes exams posed a significant challenge—historically, testing boards have been resistant to granting accommodations. In 2011, a Yale medical student with severe dyslexia took legal action against the U.S. Medical Licensing Examination board, ultimately winning a settlement that forced them to provide extra time. His case set a precedent, highlighting the systemic barriers neurodivergent students face and the lengths they must go to for basic support.

Change is happening, slowly but surely. The fight for accommodations in medical education and practice has gained momentum, pushed forward by legal battles, advocacy groups, and the voices of neurodivergent physicians who refuse to be sidelined. More medical schools are reassessing their standards, incorporating inclusive teaching strategies, and recognizing that talent doesn't always fit into rigid molds. The Association of American Medical Colleges and groups like the Coalition for Disability Access in Health Science Education are pushing for reform.[63] Medical schools are rethinking their technical standards, making room for assistive technology, alternative

[62] Meeks, L. M., & Herzer, K. R. (2016). Prevalence of self-disclosed disability among medical students in US allopathic medical schools. *JAMA, 316*(21), 2271–2272. https://doi.org/10.1001/jama.2016.10544

[63] Association of American Medical Colleges. Assist students with disabilities [Internet]. Washington, DC: AAMC. Available from: https://www.aamc.org/professional-development/affinity-groups/gsa/webinars/assist-students-with-disabilities

techniques, and structured support in clinical settings. Faculty training programs are growing, teaching instructors how to recognize neurodivergence, how to teach in ways that reach more students, and how to make space for different ways of thinking.

Supporting neurodivergent doctors isn't a one-size-fits-all approach. The right accommodations depend on the individual—what works for one physician may not work for another. While research on best practices remains limited, experts and neurodivergent physicians themselves have highlighted key strategies that could make medical training and practice more inclusive. Daniel Robinson, a psychiatry trainee with ADHD, emphasizes the need for diverse role models in senior positions, ensuring trainees can see themselves reflected in leadership. Timely feedback is another crucial element, allowing doctors to adjust their approach in real time rather than struggling with delayed evaluations. Teaching strategies that make the thought process behind complex tasks explicit—rather than leaving trainees to infer them—can also provide clarity, helping neurodivergent learners process and engage more effectively.[64]

The goal isn't just accommodations—it's something bigger. A shift from one-time fixes to a system designed with inclusion in mind. A future where neurodivergent doctors don't have to fight for scraps of support, where their skills and insights aren't just tolerated, but valued. But change is slow, and for now, too many doctors like Dr. Lockhart are still forced to make an impossible choice: push through, at

---

[64] Duong, D., & Vogel, L. (2022). Untapped potential: embracing neurodiversity in medicine. *CMAJ, 194*(27), E951–E952. https://doi.org/10.1503/cmaj.1096006

great personal cost, or walk away from the work they love.

Since leaving clinical medicine, Dr. Lockhart has stepped into work that feels both urgent and deeply personal—rebuilding organizations from the inside out, creating cultures where people don't just survive, but thrive.

She describes it simply:

Work I love, with people I love.

Now a senior faculty member and the Director of Client Engagement at Lodestar Consulting and Executive Coaching, she along with a team of colleagues help leaders and teams build workplaces where individuals can thrive—fostering connection, psychological safety, and the trust essential for healthy, sustainable cultures in the workplace.

This was the work she had been searching for. The impact she had always wanted to make. The difference she had tried, time and again, to bring to medicine. And this time, the space was there for her to do it—without fighting to be accommodated, without proving she belonged.

It hasn't just been fulfilling. It's been healing.

Someone to Blame

Dr. Nesrin Aldroubi knew exhaustion. She knew the feeling of being overwhelmed, the weight of hundreds of patients moving in and out of her care with barely enough time to ask their names. She had trained for the long hours, the endless shifts, the pressure of making life-or-death decisions in a matter of minutes.

What she hadn't trained for was fear.

She hadn't trained for the hands grabbing at her, the voices screaming in her face, the way a patient's family could turn from desperate to violent in an instant. She hadn't trained for the threats, for the way they lingered in the back of her mind long after she left the hospital. She hadn't trained for the reality that being a doctor in the pandemic didn't just mean treating the sick—it meant surviving the anger of those who didn't want to accept what medicine couldn't fix.

One night, a 90-year-old patient's oxygen levels crashed. The team moved fast, intubation tray prepped, ICU consulted. There was no hesitation, no wasted motion. Years of experience had trained her for this.

But the family didn't see it that way.

"You did something wrong!" one of them shouted.
Then another voice.

Then another step forward.

The panic turned to fury, and suddenly, they weren't just shouting—they were moving toward her.

Dr. Aldroubi barely had time to react before they were inches from her, their grief twisting into rage, their bodies tensed with blame. It wasn't the first time she had felt that fear crawl up her spine.

And it wouldn't be the last.

She thought about filing a complaint once. Thought about making it official, documenting the threats, the violence, the way her body tensed every time she stepped onto the hospital floor. But she knew what would happen. Her superiors would say it was disrespectful, that it made the hospital look bad. That it was just part of the job.

So, she stayed quiet. Like everyone else.

She remembered a gynecology resident who barely left the hospital. Thirty-eight-hour shifts, three times a week. Over and over, until exhaustion stopped being something she could fight through. One night, the resident left after a shift, got in her car, and never made it home. The accident report called it fatigue. The hospital called it tragic. The other doctors called it inevitable. Still, the work went on. Sometimes seeing hundreds, close to a thousand patients a day.

At some point, doctors stopped examining patients with mild symptoms altogether. A sore throat? Here's an antibiotic. A cough? Take this. They weren't willing to take the risk. There wasn't time to take the risk. They kept moving forward until their bodies refused to.

One night, in the middle of another chaotic shift, Dr. Aldroubi hesitated. She needed to intubate a patient. She had done it before, years ago, but fatigue made it difficult. The chaos around her felt suffocating. She turned to a nurse. "I haven't done this in six or seven years." The nurse didn't judge. He just stepped in.

That night, he was the one who saved a life. Not hospital management. Not leadership. Just colleagues keeping each other afloat, hoping it would be enough. But the shift ended. And the fear, the exhaustion, the weight of it all didn't go away. It followed her home. It reshaped the way she saw medicine.

She wasn't alone. Over 99% of physicians in Turkey report verbal abuse by patients.[65] Across the world, thousands of healthcare workers carried the same wounds—some visible, others buried deep. They were doctors, nurses, paramedics, respiratory therapists. Some had been shoved, slapped, punched.[66] Others had been threatened, screamed at, called murderers. They all walked into work the next day anyway. But not all of them stayed.

The trauma didn't end when the pandemic did. The abuse didn't just push doctors like Dr. Aldroubi to their limits—it

---

[65] Sabak M, Al-Hadidi A, Oktay MM, Al B, Kazaz T, Kowalenko T, Hakmeh W. Workplace violence in emergency departments in Turkey. Avicenna J Med. 2021 Aug 13;11(3):111-7. doi: 10.1055/s-0041-1732284. PMID: 34646787; PMCID: PMC8500074.

[66] Ma PF, Thomas J. Workplace violence in healthcare. [Updated 2023 Apr 23]. In: StatPearls Treasure Island (FL): StatPearls Publishing; Available from: https://www.ncbi.nlm.nih.gov/books/NBK592384/

pushed them out. Some walked away from medicine entirely, unable to endure the constant fear, the exhaustion, the feeling of being under attack by the very people they were trying to save. Others stayed, but not unchanged. They withdrew from patients. Avoided difficult conversations. Spoke in clipped, rehearsed explanations instead of taking the time to comfort grieving families. Medicine is built on trust. But what happens when doctors start fearing the very people they are meant to heal?

Many doctors began to emotionally detach from patients as a protective mechanism. Some hesitated to give bad news, fearing a violent reaction. Instead of open discussions, they gave short, distant explanations. Over time, implicit bias formed—doctors who had been assaulted began unconsciously labeling certain patients or families as “difficult” or “dangerous.” The public’s trust in healthcare eroded. Patients saw rushed, distant physicians who seemed uninterested in their care—when in reality, those physicians were just trying to survive their shifts. Medicine is supposed to be built on care and connection. But when doctors have to focus on self-preservation, that connection is the first thing to go.

The most dangerous part of violence in healthcare isn’t that it happens—it’s that it is tolerated. Hospitals prioritized reputation over worker safety, discouraging complaints about violence. Doctors feared retaliation if they spoke out—some worried about losing their jobs, being seen as “difficult,” or even facing legal consequences if an incident escalated. The expectation was clear: endure it. Don’t escalate it. Don’t fight back.

If we want to prevent another generation of physicians from experiencing the same violence, burnout, and system failure, we must start in medical school. Most medical students are not warned about workplace violence. They study physiology, pathology, and pharmacology, but no one tells them they might be attacked during a shift. They learn how to recognize heart failure, how to diagnose infections, how to stitch wounds closed—but they are never told what to do when a patient throws a punch.

We need to include workplace violence education in medical training, so students aren't blindsided by aggression from patients or families. They need to hear real cases—students should listen firsthand to physicians who have experienced violence and how they handled it. They should be taught their rights—what protections exist, what policies should be in place, what they can do when they are threatened.

Dr. Aldroubi knew why so many doctors left. She understood the ones who walked away, the ones who decided they couldn't take the violence, the fear, the exhaustion anymore. She wasn't sure if anyone planned to fix it.

But she knew one thing: if the system refused to protect its own, future doctors needed to be ready to protect themselves.

Playing Games with Patients

The COVID-19 pandemic shifted how we delivered care to patients as PTs. We had to teach patients how to assess their bodies because we could not examine them. We could no longer get information about patients from our hands. We had to rely on patient information and interpretation solely on what they felt and how they chose to verbalize it.

Before the pandemic, using telehealth in physical therapy was a far-fetched idea due to the profession's hands-on nature. Interestingly, though, the number of physical therapists (PTs) providing telehealth consultations increased dramatically after the pandemic began. PTs who provide evaluation and treatments to help patients recover from injury or illness had to develop engaging ways to provide the best care through telehealth. Dr. Jacquelyn Ruen, a physical therapist specializing in the lower and upper extremity issues toward preventative care, shed light on her challenges as a clinician and educator due to the pandemic.

PTs spend ample time getting to know their patients and acquiring their history, including how their lives usually functioned before the disease or injury and how it has been impacted afterward. With the shift to telehealth, this skill took on even greater importance in gaining insight into the patient's condition when unable to complete a hands-on examination. Similarly, Dr. Ruen relied more heavily on her observational and listening skills to understand a patient's experience. Dr. Ruen always aspired to educate and empower her patients about their bodies so they could have a more active, well-informed understanding of their condition and contribute to their treatment.

One of the biggest challenges Dr. Ruen faced in her practice was the lack of physical contact with the patient. She had to rely significantly on the patient's interpretation of their pain. Recognizing and assessing pain is always a challenge because many patients cannot effectively communicate how they feel. Pain is a highly personal experience that varies considerably based on social, economic, and physical factors. For example, many people are uncomfortable when expressing their pain because they have been taught to keep their struggles and trauma to themselves. They find it difficult to trust others, even their healthcare providers.

In a typical scenario, Dr. Ruen would start by observing the patient's movement patterns when she used telehealth. For instance, when evaluating an upper extremity or upper back concern, she would instruct the patient to raise their arms in different positions. When looking at the lower body, she may observe them walking and balancing on one leg to see their physical functional strength. There were times when Dr. Ruen instructed the patient to stand far away from the camera to see their entire body or place the camera closely to look at individual body part movements one at a time to get a complete and clear picture.

After assessing movement, she measured motion restrictions and tested strength. Often, she asked the patient to hold their body at a specific position and then push the same body part toward a different position. Many PTs, including Dr. Ruen, did this to see if the patient felt pain or weakness in a specific body part; they observed the patient's facial expressions with their movements to assess them. For instance, she would ask a patient to go to the kitchen and grab a box of cookies from the top cabinet. She noticed how it was easier for patients to attempt to perform such tasks to express their pain rather than try to describe it themselves.

Even though COVID-19 brought many obstacles to completing physical therapy, it also allowed many patients to see how vital physical therapy is in their day-to-day lives. Physical therapy may help patients avoid surgery. It can also allow the aging population to maintain mobility and more control over their bodies. When the pandemic struck, many people refrained from going to hospitals for minor surgeries and sought alternatives such as physical therapy to get help. For instance, Dr. Ruen had a thirteen-year-old patient who wanted to skateboard after an injury. However, the young teenager was camera shy and had zoom fatigue. They also faced distractions from a younger sibling during their physical therapy sessions. The most formidable challenge was to create a space in which the patient felt comfortable engaging in different activities and help them see their progress after each session.

My team and I considered games and activities that caught their interest during the sessions. After each session, they developed strength and could move faster in general. We also incorporated their younger sibling into the session to make it more interactive and fun. We did different balance exercises with both of them. After each session, the patient could see their movement and posture differences. They enjoyed the therapy so much that they became sad when it was finished. They had a newfound appreciation for physical therapy.

Alongside the difficulties in managing patient health, people were asked to quarantine in their homes to prevent the spread of the virus. Staying at home alone increases the likelihood of exacerbating psychological and social problems. Our social interactions are essential to our development, growth, and health. When we are deprived of socializing and meeting loved ones, it can have a psychological impact. Without regular interaction, people tend to miss smiling at strangers, greeting colleagues, bumping into an old acquaintance at a cafe, or thanking that lunch lady for the extra bagel.

These small interactions with strangers helped individuals feel part of a larger community. They provided a sense of belonging amidst a stressful, chaotic life.

An example of one of these social interactions is described as follows. Dr. Ruen had an older patient with health comorbidities and environmental irritancy issues who chose to do telephone visits during the pandemic, being overwhelmed by the idea of navigating a video session. Doing physical therapy sessions with her over the phone was extremely difficult. Still, by interacting with her regularly, Dr. Ruen realized that the patient likely felt lonely and needed someone to listen to her in addition to her physical needs. People who did not have a strong network of people required a greater degree of emotional support.

I was also able to establish strong connections with patients because I was very vocal to them about my struggles. For example, I am immunocompromised, so my risk of catching COVID-19 is also higher than many of my colleagues. I got a lot of appreciation from my patients for accepting that I was at high risk, and telehealth allowed me to still perform my work. It motivated them to fight the pandemic, too.

In these uncertain times, the COVID-19 pandemic forced PTs like Dr. Ruen to adapt to telehealth, making it an important tool for patient health. It showed patients and providers how important social interactions, as small or short as they may be, are and how important human connections are in healthcare. Dr Ruen's approach and empathy allowed her to maintain strong patient relationships, provide care, and add meaning and warmth to the lives of her patients.

Assessing pain remotely requires careful attention to how patients describe their symptoms, as pain is a subjective experience influenced by a range of personal, social, and psychological factors. As Dr. Ruen noted, some patients find it difficult to express their pain or may downplay their symptoms due to societal or cultural norms around expressing discomfort. A 2020 study published in *Pain* confirmed that pain assessment in telehealth settings is challenging without the ability to "touch, press, examine, and move patients."[67] However, the study presents an approach that can solve this challenge, citing that patient interviews can be conducted before the appointment to gather more information and educate the patient about expectations.

---

[67] Tauben DJ, Langford DJ, Sturgeon JA, Rundell SD, Towle C, Bockman C, et al. Optimizing telehealth pain care after COVID-19. Pain. 2020 Nov;161(11):2437–45.

In the end, telehealth wasn't perfect, but it was something. It was proof that care didn't end just because the world shut down. It was a reminder that healing isn't always about touch—it's about trust, about connection, about someone on the other side of the screen saying, I see you. Keep going.

A Transition from Medicine to Writing and Teaching

The pandemic pushed me to accept that I must take risks to grow. In my 20s, I was a perfectionist. In medical school, this appeared as a fear of making mistakes. The time I spent with myself in lockdown made me realize that we will always have holes in our knowledge base. The best approach was to remain curious and develop a practice that supported my creative freedom.

During the pandemic, Dr. Christopher Cirino, an infectious disease specialist, embarked on a self-discovery journey to explore his interests in writing and teaching. Even though he took pride in being a healthcare provider and supporting his patients, he faced various professional challenges that made him realize he wanted a break from corporate medicine and helped him discover new avenues to serve people. As an infectious disease physician working during the pandemic, Dr. Cirino felt trapped in his job and had to face his fear of making mistakes when his hospital administration questioned his decision-making and recommendations.

During the pandemic, Dr. Cirino experienced a massive decrease in workload. Most days, he saw between two and five patients. A significant source of consultations came from the surgery department, and the hospital's elective surgeries were canceled or deferred until later. Due to this drop in his workload, he realized he could not generate enough profit for the hospital, leaving him in fear of losing his job and developing burnout.

I had a practice disagreement with a referring physician about how a consultation was conducted. Within two days' notice, I received a call from a healthcare recruiter that they were looking for a locum tenen (temporary) physician to fill an infectious disease position at my hospital. I realized it was for my job. I had been there for 3.5 years, and I was close to being nudged out without prior notice by the hospital administration.

Unfortunately, many hospital administrations could easily replace an employed physician even after years of hard work. After that incident, I realized that the closed door opened an opportunity for me to find a pathway that could provide me with an income and free time to work on my writing.

After departing from his job, Dr. Cirino decided he wanted to do something new, which was only possible once he broke free from the fear of failure. The lockdown pushed him to introspect and take risks, which he avoided earlier in his career. In his attempt to rediscover himself, Dr. Cirino invested time combining his passion for medicine with writing and teaching. After thoroughly researching different topics, he wrote health articles on his website, Your Health Forum—providing information regarding the pandemic.

I love writing. It is a gift that can be given to others who can seamlessly connect with you based on what you have written. I always want people to understand the underlying message behind my writing.

Dr. Cirino sees his career and passions as more than just achievements or failures—they are pathways to deeper understanding. For him, learning isn't just about gaining knowledge; it's about expanding what's possible. The unknown isn't something to fear but something to explore, a space where growth happens. He believes that when we fixate on failure, fear takes over, keeping us from taking the risks that lead to real progress. Instead, he urges us to see mistakes not as setbacks but as stepping stones—each one pushing us beyond our current limits, shaping us into something stronger, something more.

Think about Thomas Edison's invention of the light bulb. If he had given up after the first 100 iterations, he would not have been its inventor.

Dr. Cirino describes how important it is to get past the idea of pleasure and instant reward. He explains that if unrealistic expectations of reaping success are unmet, we get disappointed and give up. He reminds us that many refuse to try something new and unconventional because they fear how people will react if they fail.

People want instant success to reap all the benefits. Once you let go of the idea of the result, your passions and interests become an expression of freedom beyond pain and pleasure.

The human mind often focuses on the result. Instead of focusing on the outcome, it is worth focusing on the journey and how each step serves as a pavement to learn something new. Every mistake is a stepping stone to becoming a better version of ourselves. Mistakes can be inspiring when we apply what we learn to our following attempts. Dr. Cirino's narrative depicts that we are responsible for our choices.

When Dr. Cirino changed jobs during the pandemic, he took full responsibility for the risks and moved forward into a new phase of his life. He used the lockdown period as his biggest strength to explore his inner interests. Dr. Cirino created a vision of helping others during those challenging times.

Despite his setbacks, he published four children's books and completed his first nonfiction book, *Becoming Tomorrow's Doctor*, in September 2022. This book is a reference for pre-medical students planning to enter the field of medicine. He will also launch a second book, *Journey to Wellness: Unlocking the Laws of Natural Healing*. In this book, he will discuss a holistic approach to healing from chronic disease. Moving forward, he hopes to establish a private clinic to address chronic diseases with a healing paradigm. He will continue his career in writing and speaking to inspire people to take risks without being fixated on the outcome.

A Plant-Based Diet

If you put diesel fuel in a gasoline engine, it would be a disaster. The spark plugs would clog with carbon deposits, fuel lines would sludge up, and the catalytic converter would be destroyed. The same holds true for our bodies. Many diseases that Western medicine treats—obesity, high blood pressure, type 2 diabetes, clogged arteries—are simply signs of putting the wrong fuel into our "metabolic engines."

Dr. Michael Klaper, a physician and health educator, advocates for plant-based diets to promote health and prevent disease. He encourages patients and fellow doctors to harness the healing power of plant-based foods, which he sees as key to nurturing health.

Speaking about the benefits of the plant-based diet, he notes that humans share similar digestive systems with gorillas, who thrive on plant-based diets of leaves, fruits, and occasional grubs—building strong, muscular bodies without developing chronic diseases like clogged arteries or diabetes. Dr. Klaper suggests taking a lesson from these fellow plant-eating primates, who don't suffer from the "diseases of civilization" that impact many of us.

During the pandemic, Dr. Klaper observed that many ventilated patients who didn't survive were obese and had pre-existing conditions like diabetes and atherosclerosis. As a former anesthetist, he understood that obese patients are more challenging to intubate due to excess adipose tissue in their necks and require higher ventilation pressures, which increases the risk of lung complications. He attributes these risks to the Standard American Diet (S.A.D.), which is high in meat, dairy, refined sugars, and processed foods.

Working to address these issues, Dr. Klaper became a diplomate of the American College of Lifestyle Medicine, and he understands that the six components of lifestyle medicine, including restorative sleep, daily physical activity, strong social support, avoidance of substances like tobacco and alcohol, and managing stress play essential roles in staying healthy and overcoming diseases.

1. **Whole, Plant-Based Nutrition** – A diet rich in nutrient-dense, anti-inflammatory foods supports heart health, reduces disease risk, and fuels the body for long-term well-being.
2. **Restorative Sleep** – Quality sleep is essential for immune function, cellular repair, and cognitive health, reducing stress and inflammation.
3. **Daily Physical Activity** – Regular movement strengthens the heart, improves metabolism, and enhances mental resilience.
4. **Social Connection** – Strong relationships boost emotional well-being and lower the risk of chronic disease.
5. **Avoidance of Harmful Substances** – Limiting tobacco, alcohol, and drugs preserves organ function and prevents early aging.
6. **Stress Management** – Mindfulness, meditation, and breathwork help regulate cortisol levels and combat disease.

Dr. Klaper knows that telling people to overhaul their diets overnight is a losing battle. Change—real, lasting change—doesn't happen all at once. It has to be eased into, folded into daily life in a way that sticks.

For patients struggling to give up meat, he didn't push absolutes. Instead, he encouraged them to start small—cutting back to just a few times a week, letting the body and mind adjust before taking the next step. The goal was always full commitment, but he understood that the road there wasn't always straight.

He compares it to quitting smoking. Going from two packs a day to one is better—but better wasn't the same as good. A pack a day still does damage, just like a diet still dependent on animal products keeps disease risk alive. Partial changes yield partial results. The real transformation—the real healing—only comes with full commitment.

Beyond diet, Dr. Klaper warns of the negative health effects of social isolation and excessive stress. He advises patients to seek support from health professionals who understand how to optimize lifestyle factors and can help us accordingly.

Dr. Klaper believes that, "Health comes from healthy living. Don't let stress keep your cortisol levels high, which opens the door to disease—we're here to love, learn, laugh, and support each other. Eat nourishing foods, manage stress with care, do good work, and you'll see things improve."

Now, Dr. Klaper dedicates his time to educating medical students and physicians on the life-changing potential of plant-based diets to prevent and reverse chronic diseases like obesity, heart disease, and diabetes. To learn more about his work through the non-profit Moving Medicine Forward initiative, visit www.Movingmedforward.org.

Summary and Reflection

Like a house with patched-up windows, our healthcare system showed its frailties under the onslaught of a global crisis. Where once everyone stumbled along, confident that yesterday's protocols would hold steady for tomorrow, the pandemic shattered the old assumptions and forced us to adapt on the fly. But adaptation is more than mastering a new technique or memorizing fresh guidelines; it's about rethinking the very nature of learning—who gets to learn, how they learn, and how institutions can either nurture that growth or stifle it.

In this new reality, the old guard of medicine—forty-year veterans who have seen every pandemic scare since their first days of residency—stand shoulder to shoulder with fresh graduates, both navigating evolving technologies and protocols that shift by the day. If there is one lesson this period has taught us, it's that learning doesn't end when you pin a diploma to your wall or finish your hundredth rotation. Instead, learning is a continual process, a willingness to adapt, to stumble, to learn again, to admit you don't have the answer and to seek it out collaboratively.

Students just entering the field discovered that reading about procedures in a book wasn't enough; they had to practice them through a webcam, often devising new methods of observation and assessment that melded textbook medicine with real-world improvisation. In both cases, they weren't merely adding new content to their knowledge base—they were learning entirely new ways to learn. And when what's needed is creative problem-solving in the face of unexpected threats, it's this agility that can mean the difference between stagnation and innovation.

Yet we can't ignore how unequally these burdens fell. Some trainees had ready access to technology, supportive mentors, and institutions willing to adapt. Others found themselves locked out of these resources entirely, wrestling with financial strain, biased gatekeepers, or learning needs that went unrecognized. These inequities reflect larger truths about how healthcare—and society at large—operates. If we want to build a system that can pivot quickly in a crisis, we need to ensure that every learner, whether they stand at the threshold of their career or decades beyond it, can take part in the reinvention process.

For individuals, that means embracing the idea that mastery is never static. Skills aren't trophies we collect and shelve; they're stepping stones that lead us to question, explore, and refine. For institutions, it demands a deeper shift—investing in flexible formats, ensuring the well-being of students and professionals alike, and recognizing that a one-size-fits-all model shortchanges everyone. And for policymakers, it means passing legislation that lowers financial and logistical barriers, incentivizes diverse participation, and guarantees that all who enter the field have a fair shot at thriving.

Our world keeps moving forward, and what feels like a major threat today may become a mere footnote in history tomorrow. But if the recent turmoil has taught us anything, it's that learning can't be restricted to content; it must also evolve in structure and method. We can't afford to simply "go back" to the old ways. The only path forward is one that champions constant reinvention, embraces the unique vantage points of every professional, and provides equitable access for those whose entry point is burdened by systemic inequities. In doing so, we stand a better chance of building a healthcare system that is robust, nimble, and capable of truly serving the needs of our ever-changing world.

Discussion Questions

1. How can institutions and policymakers ensure that all learners—regardless of socioeconomic status, geographical location, or learning style—have equitable access to new learning methods, technologies, and support systems?

2. What are some effective strategies for moving beyond the traditional lecture-based model of healthcare education, and how can these innovative approaches be scaled to benefit both trainees and long-practicing professionals?

3. In what ways can healthcare education be restructured to recognize and accommodate different cognitive styles, cultural backgrounds, and personal circumstances, without compromising academic rigor?

4. How can leaders at all levels (individuals, institutions, and policymakers) cultivate a culture that values ongoing learning and flexible problem-solving—rather than seeing knowledge as something you acquire once and never revisit?

5. Many shifts in healthcare education occurred rapidly during the pandemic. Which of these adaptations should be preserved or expanded, and what strategies can help sustain meaningful reform once the immediate crisis has passed

Part 6: The Overlooked Populations in Healthcare

Prisoners and Family Members of Professionals

Introduction

When a crisis strikes, its tremors rarely land in the same way for everyone. One family might agonize over letting their daughter take a job at a hospital—fearful of the virus that lurks in each corner, yet aware that turning down the job means stalling her dream. Another group, locked behind high walls and razor wire, watches the pandemic spread through cramped cells, powerless to protect themselves. Two worlds that rarely meet, but both held hostage by a healthcare system that was never built to handle everyone's needs all at once.

In neighborhoods where individual choice is prized and parents preach "follow your dreams," young people aim for careers in medicine, forging ahead despite the risks. Yet under many roofs, especially in collectivist communities, parents take the reins in moments of uncertainty. They worry, they issue warnings, and sometimes they forbid their children from stepping foot in crowded wards. According to one Pew Research study, a clear majority of parents in North America encourage independence, but in parts of East Asia, the family's collective well-being may overshadow personal ambition.[68] When a global pandemic rolls in, the stakes—and the tensions—rise. A mother's "don't risk your life just to rack up clinical hours" might echo louder than a father's quiet pride. These families juggle fear and hope, tradition and opportunity, each dynamic shaped by culture, finances,

[68] Pew Research Center. How people around the world view family ties in their countries [Internet]. 2019 Apr 22. Available from: https://www.pewresearch.org/global/2019/04/22/how-people-around-the-world-view-family-ties-in-their-countries/

and the looming specter of COVID-19.

Then there's the other side, a place cut off from the daily bustle of jobs and commuting: prisons, often relics of a bygone era. Some were built before the automobile—drafty stone walls with no ventilation to speak of—built to lock people away from view. When the virus showed up, it moved fast; cramped bunkhouses and narrow corridors became breeding grounds for outbreaks. And those living behind bars often bear more chronic conditions and higher rates of mental illness than the general public. Legal rulings like Estelle v. Gamble (1976)[69] established a duty to treat incarcerated individuals' medical needs, but real life rarely matches the mandate. Understaffed clinics and limited resources meant not everyone got the care they needed, and each day felt like a gamble with mortality.

Still, stories of hope flicker in the darkness. Some prison officials set up peer education efforts, sending well-respected inmates to persuade their skeptical neighbors[70]: "The vaccine isn't a trick; it's a shield." Slowly, the word spread. Vaccination rates climbed higher for a place accustomed to isolation and suspicion. Meanwhile, some families overcame cultural barriers, encouraging their kids to work the wards, too aware that in a world turned upside down, standing still could be just as risky as stepping forward. Both groups—courageous students and confined detainees—fought battles for dignity and safety. Both discovered that, in a healthcare system, you often have to

---

[69] *Estelle v. Gamble*, 429 U.S. 97 (1976).

[70] Mitchell MM, Seth A, Richmond A, Hickson DA, Young L, Young S, et al. Know better, live better: Community and correctional peer education for health equity in the COVID-19 era. *Am J Public Health*. 2022;112(S8):S771-S774. Available from: https://pmc.ncbi.nlm.nih.gov/articles/PMC9591706/

improvise your own solutions.

These chapters capture the divide: anxious parents deciding whether to release their children into a battlefield they can't fully see, and incarcerated individuals reliant on a prison healthcare apparatus that many on the outside don't believe should even exist. While their realities are dissimilar in almost every way—one shaped by parental caution and personal aspiration, the other by legal barriers and physical confinement—they share a hidden thread: each group's sense of vulnerability was magnified by a crisis that tested every assumption we had about fairness and access to care.

By looking closely at their stories, we see how a pandemic doesn't just threaten our lungs; it challenges the structures we've built. It forces families into hard choices and pushes prisons into impossible corners. But we also see that through compassion, ingenuity, and listening to the people most affected, solutions—however imperfect—begin to form. And maybe, through these parallel tales of aspiring healers and long-forgotten inmates, we can catch a glimpse of how healthcare, from the everyday clinic to the highest levels of policy, might one day account for those it has so often overlooked.

Worried Parents

I remember when I was interviewing for a Certified Nursing Assistant position. The employer asked if I was comfortable working with COVID-19 patients. I said yes, but deep down, I was terrified, and I didn't want to admit that because I might not get the job. PA schools require clinical hours, and I needed them.

Media platforms worldwide depicted the stories of our frontline workers, but few supported ambitious students struggling to secure opportunities during the pandemic. This was the case for pre-health students like Daren and Carolina, who felt compelled to hide their fears to achieve opportunities that could be gateways to their dreams.

As they began interviewing for jobs, they remembered the dangers of working in healthcare, especially during a pandemic. They recalled the idea of exposing themselves to a deadly virus. They wondered if it was better to continue to quarantine until conditions improved or begin working and gaining experience. In addition to this problem, they also had worried parents who debated whether to expose their children to the virus for a career opportunity or delay work temporarily.

My parents told me that I could not work. They said there would be many opportunities, but this was not the time for me to work. They told me to wait until everything became normal to find clinical opportunities. I understood their fear but realized I could not escape this situation. This was going to be a part of our lives. I had to face it and get involved.

Daren and Carolina had experiences like these while figuring out what they wanted for their careers. They once had a patient with cerebral palsy who faced many physical challenges despite being intellectually aware of his surroundings. It was particularly difficult for him because, in addition to having COVID-19, he couldn't receive the one-on-one care he needed. Carolina vividly remembers him repeatedly calling for help, but due to his speech difficulties, no one could understand him. It was heartbreaking because, while he needed someone to take the time to listen and understand him, the overwhelming number of patients made it nearly impossible to provide the individual attention he deserved. These experiences greatly impacted the decisions of the students about their professions.

Stories like these during the pandemic have a massive influence on the trajectories of pre-health students all over the globe. These students saw the harsh realities of a healthcare worker's lifestyle. Despite knowing the risks of working in healthcare during a pandemic, students like Daren and Carolina bravely served alongside other healthcare professionals. We applaud them for their bravery. As we have seen, the pandemic highlighted the positive and negative aspects of the medical industry, motivating many pre-health students to pursue this noble profession while convincing others to choose a different one.

One study revealed that "the pandemic-affected job market has resulted in a large proportion of graduates thinking differently about their futures (79.4%) and facing greater challenges finding employment than they expected (71.9%). A large majority of participants either agreed (25.5%) or strongly agreed (48.3%) that they noticed a fall

in the number of available opportunities. Over two thirds agree (24.9%) or strongly agree (43.9%) that they have found it a challenge to find graduate jobs they want to apply for and agree (32.9%) or strongly agree (31.3%) that they have found the recruitment process challenging, whilst few (17.7%) have felt supported by employers through the recruitment process."[71]

The study highlighted a difficult reality—many graduates struggled to find employment, facing limited job openings, a lack of support during the application process, and uncertainty about their career prospects. The economic downturn made it challenging for them to secure positions in their desired fields, leaving many feeling lost as they stepped into the workforce.

Addressing job availability for graduates during crises like a global pandemic requires a thoughtful, multi-layered approach. Strengthening collaboration between universities, local governments, and industries can help create job placement programs that align with market needs. Healthcare organizations offering subsidized or virtual internships can provide hands-on experience, even in remote settings, making professional development more accessible. Similarly, wage subsidies or stimulus programs, like those implemented in Australia and Canada during the pandemic,

[71] Tomlinson M, Reedy F, Burg D. Graduating in uncertain times: The impact of COVID -19 on recent graduate career prospects, trajectories and outcomes. Higher Education Quarterly. 2023 Jul;77(3):486–500.

can encourage hiring and provide stability for recent graduates.[72]

By integrating these strategies, the transition from education to employment can become more secure, even in uncertain times. Ensuring that graduates have access to opportunities despite economic downturns helps maintain a strong, resilient workforce.

[72] Australia Institute. *Youth Unemployment and the Pandemic: Australia* [Internet]. Canberra (AU): Australia Institute; 2022 Apr. Available from: https://australiainstitute.org.au/wp-content/uploads/2022/04/P1143-Youth-unemployment-and-pandemic-Australia-Web.pdf

An Inmate's Only Hope

During the COVID-19 pandemic, Dr. LaMenta Conway, a state administrator and deputy chief of health services for the Illinois Department of Corrections (IDOC), helped to lead the care for over 32,000 individuals in custody as the novel COVID-19 began its surge. She described the early days of the pandemic as preparing to respond to an unknown enemy that caused tremendous havoc and invaded the lives of many individuals in prison.

I remember the terrifying feeling when we had little information on how to manage COVID-19 in prison and who would provide care. The first people affected by the virus were dialysis patients in one of our Chicago area facilities.

To better serve the inmates, she and her team assembled a team to monitor each unit, safely move susceptible patients, and educate and convince inmates to wear masks and wash their hands frequently. When vaccines were available, the individuals in custody were also encouraged to get fully vaccinated.

Even with the brightest minds in medicine working together, there was a pervasive sense of helplessness. No one knew how many more lives the virus would claim or what the future held for vulnerable populations. Death rates in the community were soaring, and the atmosphere was turbulent.

Many prison cells housed susceptible patients, who were often deemed unworthy of healthcare by some political groups. Questions arose about why prisoners should receive vaccines alongside the general population. To combat this, Dr. Conway and the prison leadership met daily with other public health leaders to strategize how to protect prisoners from the virus and dispel conspiracy theories.

Everyone I worked with was overwhelmed by the pandemic. During one command center call, the Agency Director asked me to sing gospel music to uplift and rejuvenate the team's spirits.

Among the many challenges Dr. Conway's team faced was moving prisoners from reception centers to parent facilities, which risked spreading the virus and creating an infection catastrophe. Several prisons built in the 1800s posed additional challenges, making the situation even more dire. Due to isolation recommendations, inmates remained in reception centers longer than usual without adequate exercise or communication.

When I spoke to them, I heard how much they appreciated people like myself with leadership roles in prison. I remember them saying, "People from big offices do not come down here to check on us, but you all came." We understood that many inmates had troubled pasts, but we believed they deserved fair treatment because the disease did not discriminate.

The vaccination rate in my prison facilities was around 75 percent, which was higher than most prisons. The biggest achievement for my team and I was that we were able to help them overcome their fears about healthcare and dismiss conspiracy theories about vaccines in their minds.

Instead of alienating prisoners due to their past actions, Dr. Conway and her team worked with them and saw them as human beings who needed help. She did not judge them by their criminal records; she understood their lives were filled with stories and experiences beyond their crimes. Dr. Conway realized that constantly reminding them of their past would only help grow resentment in them. Instead, she showed compassion and kindness, trying to protect them from the virus. The inmates appreciated her efforts, and through these efforts, Dr. Conway and her team made a significant impact, helping inmates create a safer future.

Despite the uncertainty, one of the approaches Dr. Conway used in managing the pandemic was her focus on vaccine hesitancy among incarcerated individuals. Many inmates, particularly from marginalized communities, were initially skeptical about receiving the COVID-19 vaccine due to a history of mistrust in the healthcare system.[73] Dr. Conway recognized this and worked to bridge the gap through authentic engagement. As a Black woman from similar communities in Chicago, she related to the prisoners' backgrounds and used her authenticity to connect with them. This personal connection is aligned with findings in vaccine hesitancy literature, which suggests that community leaders from similar cultural backgrounds can significantly improve vaccine acceptance by providing a sense of safety and trust.[74] Dr. Conway's peer educator program, where formerly incarcerated individuals and trusted inmates

[73] Ferdinand KC. Overcoming Barriers to COVID-19 Vaccination in African Americans: The Need for Cultural Humility. Am J Public Health. 2021 Apr;111(4):586–8.

[74] Ferdinand KC. Overcoming Barriers to COVID-19 Vaccination in African Americans: The Need for Cultural Humility. Am J Public Health. 2021 Apr;111(4):586–8.

promoted the vaccine, was a key strategy that led to a 75 percent vaccination rate, which was higher than many other US correctional facilities.

Dr. Conway's ability to engage with incarcerated individuals, address vaccine hesitancy, and implement peer-driven education programs led to remarkable results. As we move forward, we must build on these lessons to ensure that all vulnerable populations, including those in correctional facilities, receive equitable healthcare. The pandemic revealed the need for proactive planning, improved health communication, and policies that prioritize the well-being of incarcerated individuals. To strengthen future responses, policymakers and public health leaders must invest in community-driven interventions, ensure healthcare access in prisons, and support frontline workers like Dr. Conway.

Summary and Reflection

A crisis doesn't distribute suffering equally. It amplifies the inequalities that were already there, turning inconvenience into catastrophe for those living closest to the edge. The pandemic didn't just test our healthcare system—it exposed it. It showed us who gets care without question and who has to fight for it. It revealed how healthcare, in America and beyond, is not just about medicine but about access, privilege, and power.

For some, healthcare is a given. A job comes with insurance, a routine checkup is a minor errand, and a doctor's visit is an expectation, not a financial calculation. For others, care is precarious. A lost paycheck means a skipped appointment. A closed clinic means a worsening condition. A pandemic means making impossible choices—between safety and survival, between protecting your family and keeping your job.

When the world shut down, pre-health students desperate for experience found themselves locked out of hospitals, while essential workers with no safety net were forced to keep showing up, day after day. Parents weighed whether to let their children risk their health for career opportunities, while entire communities—low-income workers, people of color, rural residents—had little say in whether they would be exposed at all.

And then there were those already on the margins: the elderly, the incarcerated, the uninsured. People for whom healthcare was already out of reach, now further away than ever. People who, when the vaccine rollout began, weren't sure if they would even be considered. They weren't asking when they would get their shot; they were asking if they ever would.

Yet, despite the failures of the system, people found ways to adapt. Communities organized to fill in the gaps, setting up networks of mutual aid when government help was slow to arrive. Prison officials, recognizing that trust in the system was nonexistent, sent in peer educators—fellow inmates—to advocate for vaccinations. Families, despite their fears, either encouraged their children to step onto the front lines, knowing that standing still was not an option or restricted them for their own safety.

But adaptation is not the same as justice. The fact that people had to rely on informal networks to get healthcare, that essential workers had to risk their lives just to keep their jobs, that entire populations were overlooked until they fought to be noticed—that is not a triumph. It is a failure.

The pandemic was not just a medical emergency; it was a moral reckoning. It forced us to confront the gaps in our system and ask: Who gets access to care? Who is forced to go without? And why do we continue to accept a reality where some people's health is treated as optional?

The crisis may have faded, but the disparities remain. If we take nothing else from this moment, let it be this: healthcare cannot be a privilege reserved for those with the right job, the right income, or the right address. Because the next emergency will come. And if we haven't learned from this one, the same people will be left behind again.

Unless we decide, collectively, that they won't be.

Discussion Questions

1. How do economic and social determinants of health intersect with the structural failures of the healthcare system during a crisis? To what extent should healthcare policy focus on upstream social determinants (such as housing, education, and employment) versus downstream interventions (such as emergency funding and resource allocation during a crisis)?

2. In a resource-scarce environment, such as during the height of the pandemic, how should healthcare institutions ethically allocate limited supplies (e.g., vaccines, ventilators, hospital beds)? What frameworks should guide these decisions, and how can policymakers balance medical necessity with social justice concerns?

3. The pandemic forced pre-health students, medical trainees, and early-career professionals into high-risk environments, often with little institutional support. What ethical responsibilities do medical institutions and employers have to ensure the safety and informed consent of those entering the workforce in crisis conditions?

4. How can ethical frameworks such as utilitarianism, deontology, and virtue ethics be applied to future public health decision-making? Are there new ethical paradigms that should emerge in response to

the unique moral challenges posed by global pandemics?

5. Should hazard pay, guaranteed sick leave, or other protections be legally mandated for essential healthcare workers in future public health emergencies? What are the potential economic and ethical trade-offs of such policies?

Conclusion

Covering topics rampant in the COVID-19 pandemic, this book aimed to cover themes revealed through interviews and organize them into narratives for its readers. As you read these narratives, we hope you gained a newfound understanding of the difficulties faced during the pandemic. Although these stories could not capture the entire pandemic experience, they offer a small yet valuable glimpse into life during the COVID-19 pandemic, which changed many of our lives.

The pandemic took away our loved ones and caused financial setbacks, allowing reform to our healthcare system and letting us introspect on our dreams and aspirations. Some of us found new ways to move forward and make progress during the pandemic, and others were left wondering about how to move forward. Some found new business ventures, met amazing new people, picked up new hobbies, and are reaping the benefits of these outcomes. Unfortunately, some faced financial setbacks, lost beloved people, became inconsistent with hobbies they once loved, and now suffer due to these circumstances. The pandemic served as a wake-up call for us all to take advantage of the blessings and opportunities we have available, to hold fast to what matters, and to put effort into nurturing relationships with loved ones before we lose them.

To those reading who tirelessly worked in jobs healthcare-related and not, who have lost family, friends, and other loved ones, suffered from COVID-19, loneliness, addiction, lost their jobs, found it difficult juggling their responsibilities, and many more struggles, all of which are too great to list, we applaud you for your strength and efforts. We are happy for the growth you have shown thus far and are proud of you. We thank you all for your service and dedicate this book to you. We hope this book serves as a testament to your sacrifice, efforts, and excellent work in helping the people around you.

About the Authors

Ramsha Essa graduated from Loyola University Chicago with a Bachelor's in Software Engineering and Film and Digital Media. She currently works as a software developer while pursuing a Master's degree in Information Systems and Entrepreneurship. Ramsha wrote this book to highlight the inspiring stories of healthcare providers who have made incredible sacrifices to serve people worldwide. When she's not writing, she enjoys performing in short films and web series, exploring her passion for acting. In addition to acting, Ramsha loves writing fiction and creating career guidance videos for young professionals. She is dedicated to empowering South Asian women to achieve financial independence and pursue their dreams. Outside of her professional pursuits, she enjoys being on camera and staying physically fit through her workout routine.

Mirza Mustafa Baig is a third-year medical student at Kansas City University College of Osteopathic Medicine and graduated from Loyola University Chicago with a Bachelor's degree in Molecular Biology. He wrote this book to educate future generations about the challenges medical professionals faced during the pandemic, aiming to raise awareness about their sacrifices and various important issues. When he is not writing, Mirza enjoys spending time with family and friends, staying active at the gym, and volunteering, where he gains hands-on experience and engages with his community. An avid learner and through his work and outreach, Mirza hopes to make a lasting impact on the public, particularly on students and the next generation of healthcare providers.

About Pre-Health Shadowing

Pre-Health Shadowing (PHS) is a non-profit organization that emerged from a unique need during a critical moment in history. Founded in 2020 during the height of the COVID-19 pandemic, PHS was created to provide aspiring healthcare professionals with remote shadowing opportunities when traditional, in-person experiences were no longer an option. What started as a response to a global crisis quickly grew into a sustainable solution for students across the world.

PHS has since evolved into a vital platform that bridges the gap between healthcare education and accessibility. Our mission is to make learning opportunities in healthcare more inclusive, addressing barriers like geographic limitations, financial constraints, and limited access to mentors. We provide a flexible, virtual environment where students from all walks of life can gain real-world insight into various healthcare fields by connecting with professionals in the industry.

With over 70,000 students impacted, PHS continues to empower the next generation of healthcare leaders, offering them a chance to gain critical experience, build networks, and pursue their passion for medicine—no matter where they are.

Meet the Contributors

Nina Bouzamondo-Bernstein
Pre-Health Shadowing
Founder & CEO

Nina graduated from University of California, Santa Barbara with a biopsychology degree and is the founder and CEO of Pre-Health Shadowing.

Alina Azmat
Project Coordinator

Alina graduated from the University of Waterloo with a Bachelor of Science in Health Science and continued her educational journey to become a Naturopathic Doctor at the Canadian College of Naturopathic Medicine.

Jennifer Abayowa
Editor

Jennifer graduated from Howard University and is a freelance medical writer and editor who creates content for healthcare brands. She has worked with many Fortune 500 companies, including Johnson & Johnson, P&G, and Medline.

Eric Lindberg
Editor

Eric is an editor and writer with nearly 20 years of experience. He graduated from USC Annenberg with a degree in print journalism and has worked in higher education, contributed to peer-reviewed publications, and earned awards as a staff writer.

Kai Miller
Illustrator

Kai is a graphic designer and marking specialist with a BFA in Graphic Design and minor in Marketing from California State University Long Beach.

Kira Charlton
Illustrator

Kira is a pre-med student at California State University, Fullerton, with interests in psychiatry, neurology, and psychology.

Dr. Sunshine (Sunny) Nakae
Pre-Health Shadowing Advisory Board Member

Dr. Nakae is the Senior Associate Dean for Equity, Inclusion, Diversity, and Partnership at California University of Science and Medicine. She has held roles in admissions and diversity at UC Riverside, Loyola University Chicago, Northwestern, and the University of Utah. She holds a BS, MSW, and PhD in Higher Education, and is the author of *Premed Prep: Advice from a Medical School Admissions Dean.*

premedprepadvice@gmail.com

Meet the Team

Meet the team who brought this book to life. While this project involved over 40 team members, we're excited to showcase just a few of them here.

May Rajtboriraks
Creative Design Lead

Ameera Khan
Instagram Co-Lead

Maria Abdelmeish
Instagram Co-Lead

Tatiana Cubes-Hernandez
TikTok Lead

Ashley Shen
Marketing Team Member

Adriana Camila
Research Team Member

Ziwen Qian
Marketing Team Member

Enoch Gurah Anosh
Social Media Team Member

Fatima Khan Lookmanji
Editorial Team Member

Aabha Vadapalli
Marketing Team Member

Gehna Srivastava
Marketing Team Member

Sidona Berhe
Social Media Team Member

Yulia Dubrovensky
Social Media Team Member

Ayesha Haider
Social Media Team Member

Charlie Sconiers
Authors Communication Lead

Abinaya Sridharan
Marketing Team Member

Fatima Atieh
Research Team Member

Kevin Brain
Research Team Member

www.ingramcontent.com/pod-product-compliance
Lightning Source LLC
LaVergne TN
LVHW012315160826
845684LV00042B/27

9798988904106